Copyright © 2024 by Paper Crown Publishing

All rights reserved.

No portion of this book may be reproduced in any form without written permission from the publisher or author, except as permitted by U.S. and U.K. copyright law.

ISBN 978-1-7385716-3-5

Paper Crown Publishing
Paper Crown Media Ltd
71-75 Shelton Street
Covent Garden, London WC2H 9JQ

Scripture quotations marked (NIV) are taken from the Holy Bible, New International Version®, NIV®. Copyright © 1973, 1978, 1984, 2011 by Biblica, Inc.™ Used by permission of Zondervan. All rights reserved worldwide. www.zondervan.com

The "NIV" and "New International Version" are trademarks registered in the United States Patent and Trademark Office by Biblica, Inc.™

Scripture quotations marked (AMPCE) are taken from the Amplified Bible, Classic Edition. Copyright © 1954, 1958, 1962, 1964, 1965, 1987 by The Lockman Foundation. Used by permission.

Scripture quotations marked (TPT) are from The Passion Translation®. Copyright © 2017, 2018, 2020 by Passion & Fire Ministries, Inc. Used by permission. All rights reserved. ThePassionTranslation.com.

Scripture quotations marked (TLB) are taken from The Living Bible. Copyright © 1971 by Tyndale House Foundation. Used by permission of Tyndale House Publishers, Inc., Carol Stream, Illinois 60188. All rights reserved.

Scripture quotations marked (NLT) are taken from the Holy Bible, New Living Translation. Copyright © 1996, 2004, 2015 by Tyndale House Foundation. Used by permission of Tyndale House Publishers, Inc., Carol Stream, Illinois 60188. All rights reserved.

Scripture quotations marked (NASB) are taken from the New American Standard Bible®. Copyright © 1960, 1962, 1963, 1968, 1971, 1972, 1973, 1975, 1977, 1995, 2020 by The Lockman Foundation. Used by permission.

Scripture quotations marked (KJV) are from the King James Version of the Bible.

Scripture quotations marked (ESV) are from The Holy Bible, English Standard Version® (ESV®), copyright © 2001 by Crossway, a publishing ministry of Good News Publishers. Used by permission. All rights reserved.

Scripture quotations marked (NKJV) are taken from the New King James Version®. Copyright © 1982 by Thomas Nelson. Used by permission. All rights reserved.

Contents

Foreword	VII
1. Untangled from Doubt Meliza Farndell	1
2. Launched into Destiny Shirley Chancellor	17
3. Embraced by Love Andrea John	31
4. Come Follow Me Pamela Rice	47
5. El Roi- The God Who Sees Me Ginia Bishop	63
6. The Uncharted Uknown Kerri-Ann Luketic	73
7. How Jesus Set Me Free from Guilt and Condemnation Paula Burr	87
8. Breaking into Brokenness-Bringing Beauty Out of Ashes Cynthia Mergen	101

Coming October 2025	121
Join Paper Crown Media	123
You Are the Light	125

Foreword

Have you ever been so frustrated with trying to get God to move that you were about ready to give up on Him?

About a decade ago, I was teetering on the edge of a mental and physical breakdown. Every strategy I had employed to get God to fix me seemed fruitless.

I was doing all the good, Christian things. I attended church, read my Bible, and prayed. I even attended Bible School for a year. Nothing was working. I was a lost cause. No wonder God did not show up for me.

I told my husband: "I give up! I give up on God. He either doesn't care about me or He cannot help me. I am done!"

My wise husband remained silent, knowing I could not process anything meaningful in that moment of deep despair.

A few days later, I went to see the latest Disney movie, Tangled, with my son. He was three years old at the time. As we walked down the aisle to find our seats, I could tangibly sense the presence of the Holy Spirit.

Tears were streaming down my face, from the opening scene to the end credits. As I watched Rapunzel's story unfold, I realised I was getting a glimpse behind the scenes of my life. I, too, belonged to a Kingdom and was destined to reign. The tower was no place for me!

Like Rapunzel, I had an enemy with a vested interest in keeping me from discovering who I truly was and what was rightfully mine. However, it was the revelation of the Father's love that broke down the walls I had been building around my heart.

When I walked into the cinema, I walked straight into the heart of my Father. My life changed forever.

This encounter started the process of getting untangled from the lies keeping me stuck in my tower. It made me acutely aware of the presence of God in my everyday life. As I heard my Father speak His tender, yet powerful words of affirmation over my heart, I started to transform. Every day now holds the potential to get more untangled as I receive the Father's love and truth into my heart.

> *"For if you embrace the truth, it will release true freedom into your lives."*
>
> (John 8:32, TPT)

The journey towards freedom began for me in that place of encounter. As I continued to experience the heart of the Father, I have been able to uncover more about my identity, my inheritance, and the purpose for which I was created.

The Father often uses the images from that Disney movie, to speak to my heart or give me direction for my life.

I stood heart abandoned in worship one Sunday morning when I experienced a vision; seeing myself as a little girl at the feet of Jesus. I was making paper crowns. It was a toddler's paradise. There were fake gems, glitter, pom-poms, feathers, colourful markers, cardboard, and glue.

As soon as I finished a paper crown, I would hand it to Jesus. He was wearing these silly crowns as if they were made from the finest, rarest of treasures. Seeing the delight on His face as he donned each one, encouraged me to make even more. I couldn't make them quickly enough.

Then I saw Him hand these crowns to the Father, and the Father was sending these paper crowns into the night sky. They turned into lanterns leading His lost children home.

I knew this vision was an invitation to come into a revelation of who I was called to be. My purpose was not to be a best-selling author, even if I was doing it for the glory of God. My purpose was found at the feet of Jesus. Every story, chapter, book, or social media post I wrote was a paper crown to Him. Every paper crown was destined for a heart desperately needing the love of the Father; someone, needing to encounter His heart.

This is how Paper Crown Media Ltd was birthed. There are so many people with stories of encountering God's heart, and I am on a mission to get those lanterns out into the night sky. There are many people stuck in towers who were created for the Kingdom. They need to be called back to where they belong. Back to the arms of the Father and the freedom of the Kingdom.

In this book, you will meet some amazing writers who have stories just like mine. The Father's love is *not* conditional. There is nothing you can do to earn it. It is a gift. We are all His favourites; inimitably loved. As we encounter His love, we become a unique expression of His heart.

Dear friend, are you able to embrace the truth that the Father speaks over you? Can you hear His heartbeat for you? Do you know how deeply He loves you?

I invite you to open your heart wide as you read these stories of God encounters that will ignite your hope and build your faith. The Father wants to meet with you.

I know you will get glimpses of his heart throughout this book. Every story in the Paper Crowns Collection has been written with you in mind. Every collaborating author has been praying for you.

I pray it will illuminate every area of your heart where darkness is tormenting you. There is nothing to fear.

Your Father has you.

He loves you so much.

Welcome home.

Meliza Farndell
Director, Paper Crown Media Ltd.

Chapter One

Untangled from Doubt

Meliza Farndell

Has your heart ever been tangled up in doubt and unbelief? You want to stay in faith, but you just can't seem to marry up the hours of praying and declaring with the results you are seeing in the flesh? Have you found yourself shouting at God in sheer frustration: "You said nothing is impossible, Father! What is going on here? Where is the breakthrough we have been praying for?"

An Impossible Situation

The frustration had been building up for months. We had been standing in faith for a friend who needed a breakthrough in his work situation, and it was beginning to have a severe impact on his mental health. He was worried about losing his ability to care for his family; a beautiful wife and four young children. They had just bought a bigger home to accommodate their growing family, and the deal was not yet through. He needed an answer, and he needed it fast!

We had been praying for him in our connect group every Wednesday evening. Many of us were praying daily; desperately knocking on the Father's door, asking for a miracle. Week after week, we prayed. There seemed to be no answer. When we saw our friend, the anxiety in his heart was palpable.

My heart was in agony for him and his family. I couldn't stand it anymore. One morning, I stood over the washing basket, folding and sorting out our clean laundry. I looked out the window, and I felt a holy tantrum rising in me. I couldn't contain it anymore. God said it in His word: Nothing is impossible for Him. Why isn't He doing something about this situation?

I abandoned the pile of laundry on the bed to find my Amplified Classic Edition. I was about to go and show God what He said and ask Him to explain Himself. Turning to Luke 1:37, I read it out loud:

"For with God, nothing is ever impossible..."

"You see, Father. There it is! You said it."

And then I noticed something interesting. The scripture did not end there, it continued to say:

"...and no word from God shall be without power or impossible of fulfillment."

A rush of excitement flooded my heart. I felt like I had discovered a key to a door that had been impossible to open, and this door led to a great treasure.

There was no hope for the laundry to find its way to our wardrobes this morning. I started to follow the Father into His study, sensing He had some things to show me. Opening my Bible to the first chapter in Luke, I started to look at the key verse in context.

These were the words spoken to a young girl who was about to conceive the greatest promise there would ever be; Jesus, the Messiah, Salvation Himself; a promise that would change the entire world.

The Word was given to Mary by the angel Gabriel, a messenger from Yahweh. He carried the Word and imparted it to a young virgin. The Word implanted in her heart became flesh and dwelt among us. (See John 1:14).

As I started to unpack Mary's encounter with Gabriel, revelation flooded my heart. Revelation, which I know, will help you unlock doors previously impossible to open. Here are some keys to unlock a seemingly stuck door:

Key #1 - Miracles result from a partnership between Heaven and Earth.

Apart from the act of Creation, can you find where God decided to do something for humanity anywhere in the Bible without some conversation or partnership with humankind?

When the world became so dark and evil, to the point where God regretted creating people, there was a man who found favour in His eyes. God partnered with Noah and preserved the human race. Without Noah responding to the Word, the instructions of God, all the people of the earth would have been destroyed. (See Genesis 6).

To establish a nation, he called another man, Abraham. Abraham received a promise with a visual representation to remind Him of what God vowed to do. When he looked up to the stars, or down to his feet in the sand, he was reminded of what God had said: "You will be a father of many nations." (See Genesis 17:5).

He partnered with Joseph to bring provision.

He partnered with Moses to bring deliverance.

He partnered with Rahab to bring protection.

He partnered with Joshua to occupy the land He promised His people.

He partnered with David to rule His people.

He partnered with Solomon to build His temple where His people could worship.

He partnered with His prophets to bring vision and direction.

There was not one account where God provided, delivered, protected, occupied territory, ruled, or directed His people without their permission and participation. God will never force His will on us, we have to humble ourselves, ask, and submit to the Word (the promises and the instructions) we receive from Him.

God wants to bring salvation to the earth. He wants to bring salvation into your circumstances. Into the situations you are passionately praying for. He wants to bring solutions through you for the world around you. Will you partner with Him?

This is what Mary did when she received the Word Gabriel delivered. She partnered with God when she responded: "Let it be unto me according to your word." (See Luke 1:38).

She took herself away for the first three months as she protected and nurtured the word she received within her heart. There were no physical signs to reveal she was about to give birth to the Messiah. She only had a promise. There was no sensation of a baby kicking inside her yet.

To safeguard the incorruptible seed conceived in her heart, she surrounded herself with people of faith. Elizabeth, her cousin, was also experiencing a supernatural birth. Mary had a visual representation of the promise the Lord made to her.

Mary wrote a beautiful song, praising God for the salvation about to enter the earth through her. She sang praises to God in thanksgiving for what He was doing through the presence of Jesus on the earth. She sang this song *before* she had the baby in her arms; *before* the baby kicked in her womb.

What is the promise He has made to you? Have you responded to His promise? Do you have it in front of your eyes daily? Can you see salvation in the outcome you imagine, even before the breakthrough comes?

> "Blessed is she who has believed that the Lord would fulfill his promises to her!"
>
> Luke 1:45, NIV

Key #2 - The sovereignty of God is displayed in the principles of Creation.

We can often think it may not be God's will when we pray for salvation in a situation and it doesn't come. We put it down to the sovereignty of God. God decides who gets healed, delivered, and saved.

I have found this a very difficult reality to swallow. I know it is not an easy subject to broach, so bear with me because there may be some truth here to help you get the door to your breakthrough unjammed.

God's very nature is to heal, protect, deliver, and provide. James 1:17 in the Amplified Bible says: "Every good thing given and every perfect gift is from above; it comes down from the Father of lights [the Creator and Sustainer of the heavens], in whom there is no variation [no rising or setting] or shadow cast by His turning [for He is perfect and never changes]."

He is a good Father, and He is consistent. He doesn't choose to bless one child and not the other. He isn't going to say 'yes' to you one day, and then 'no' to you the next. All His promises are yes and amen. (See 2 Corinthians 1:20)

We never have to doubt His will for our lives. He wants us to prosper and be in good health. Always. We can be one hundred percent assured of His will in every situation. When the outcome isn't good, it is not His will. We have missed it somewhere. I am not saying we didn't have the faith we needed, but something was amiss.

The sovereignty of God is not displayed in the way He controls the outcome, but in the principles He set in motion to govern our world. Those principles (or forces) cannot be tampered with. They are incorruptible and unstoppable.

These forces are displayed in the story of Creation.

Where there is chaos, wherever things are out of order, you have a breeding ground for the miraculous. Genesis 1:2 (NIV) describes the earth as 'formless and empty, darkness was over the surface of the deep'. It is exactly there where we found the first force in operation '...and the Spirit of God was hovering over the waters.'

The second force was released when God Himself spoke the Word.

> *And God said, "Let there be light," and there was light.*
> Genesis 1:3, NIV

When Mary asked Gabriel, "How could this be?" he answered saying the Spirit of God would come upon her and He would overshadow her. (See Luke 1:35). Mary encountered both these forces, the Spirit, and the Word, and the Word became flesh within her.

Dear friend, where are you experiencing chaos right now? I want to remind you today that you have the Spirit of God living inside you (Romans 8:11). You have access to every promise in His Word. These forces are incorruptible and unstoppable. God is sovereign in the principles He has established to govern the earth.

Receive His Word, receive His Spirit, and see Salvation come through you.

Key #3 – Salvation is first conceived in your heart and then released into your circumstances.

Have you ever wondered why we are told to guard our hearts *above all else*? (See Proverbs 4:23).

I used to think guarding my heart meant not opening my heart to someone who wasn't trustworthy. But I have since discovered that it is not about keeping people out, but about what I allow to enter my heart.

Our hearts are the very seat of our being. It is the meeting point between soul and spirit. As I delved deep into Proverbs 4:23 in my Strong-Lite concordance, it became clear to me how the heart creates the boundaries within which we function. In essence, we determine the extent to which God can move within us and through us by the condition of our hearts.

Jesus illustrated this when he shared the parable of the sower. You may be familiar with the story. The sower scattered seeds on different types of soil. The soils that were harder, or full of stones and thorns, did not produce a harvest. It was the good soil, the soft and receptive soil, that offered the right environment for the seed to take root and produce a crop.

> *"Listen then to what the parable of the sower means: When anyone hears the message about the kingdom and does not understand it, the evil one comes and snatches away what was sown in their heart. This is the seed sown along the path. The seed falling on rocky ground refers to someone who hears the word and at once receives it with joy. But since they have no roots, they last only a short time. When trouble or persecution comes because of the word, they quickly fall away. The seed falling among the thorns refers to someone who hears the word, but the worries of this life and the deceitfulness of wealth choke the word, making it unfruitful. But the seed falling on good soil refers to someone who hears the word and understands it. This is the one who*

> *produces a crop, yielding a hundred, sixty, or thirty times what was sown."*
>
> Matthew 13:18-23, NIV

The condition of our hearts determines whether we receive the incorruptible seed of the Word and allow it to produce the Salvation we need.

In the first chapter of Luke, we have the same angel bringing the Word (a promise of supernatural birth) to two people–Mary and Zacharia. They both asked the same question: "How could this be?" But only one of them had a heart able to receive the promise. Gabriel had to shut Zacharia's mouth so that he could not destroy the seed of this promise with his words of doubt and unbelief. (See Luke 1:11-20).

So, dear friend, may I ask you to stop for a moment and consider this–what is the condition of your heart?

Have you hardened certain pieces of your heart because of disappointment or pain from the past? Are there some heavy rocks or thorny weeds keeping God's promises from taking root and producing the life you have been praying for?

Take a moment to invite the Holy Spirit to show you where the soil of your heart needs regeneration. Allow Him to gently remove the debris keeping the Word from growing in your heart.

All things are possible

Fresh faith rose in my heart as I poured over my Bible that morning. We needed a different strategy! We have been begging God to come and fix a situation on our behalf when He had already given us everything we needed to overcome. (See 2 Peter 1:3).

As I drove to pick up my kids from school that afternoon, I had a vision of my friend. I saw him as Peter, the valiant warrior from the Chronicles of Narnia. He was standing in his armour, sword in hand, ready to defeat the army in front of him. Not only was he winning his own battles, but he was leading the charge for his brothers and sisters.

I shared this vision with him and the group praying for him. I also shared the revelations I received that morning. We came into agreement with the truth of who God said he was. We didn't ask in desperation for God to intervene. We started speaking into his situation with the authority we were given as children of God. Things began to change.

He received a better job that suited him to a tee. It came with bigger rewards to bless his family. They moved into their dream home. His new career allowed him to pursue his dream of becoming an ordained pastor; a role he is currently enjoying.

Dear friend, I don't know what circumstances you are facing today, but I know God cares deeply about everything affecting His beloved children. He is not slow in answering your prayers. He is waiting for you to come into the knowledge of who He has created you to be. Once you realise who you are, and the authority you have as a child of God, you will discover a world where all things are indeed possible for you. You will get untangled from doubt.

START TODAY:

Find a place where you can switch off all distractions and quiet your heart.

Imagine the Father putting his arm around you and speaking gently to you:

> "My son (or daughter), pay attention to what I say; turn your ear to my words. Do not let them out of your sight, keep them within your heart; for they are life to those who find them and health to one's whole body. Above all else, guard your heart, for everything you do flows from it. Keep your mouth free of perversity; keep corrupt talk far from your lips. Let your eyes look straight ahead; fix your gaze directly before you. Give careful thought to the paths for your feet and

be steadfast in all your ways. Do not turn to the right or the left; keep your foot from evil."

Proverbs 4:20-27, NIV

The Father is with you right now, showing you the way out of the tentacles of doubt. He is not frustrated with you or tired of seeing you struggle. He has great compassion for what you are going through. He is giving you His fatherly advice in a loving, non-judgemental way.

As you continue to focus on His presence, grab your journal and make a note of what He shows you.

"PAY ATTENTION TO WHAT I SAY; TURN YOUR EAR TO MY WORDS."

Ask the Father to show you where your focus has been shifted. What were the promises He has spoken over your life?

Ask Him to give you a specific Word or a promise for the situation you have been praying about. Ask Him to give you fresh eyes to look at your problem and write down what He gives you. Make it a colourful picture, give it sound, smell the air, and feel the emotions this vision sparks in your heart.

"DO NOT LET THEM OUT OF YOUR SIGHT, KEEP THEM WITHIN YOUR HEART."

Have you lost sight of the Words and the promises the Father has spoken over your life? Ask Him to help you find a way to plant these incorruptible, life-producing seeds deep into your heart.

Build these truths into your daily habits. Can you write them down and put them where you can see them often? On your bedside table, your bathroom mirror, next to the kettle, on the lid of the cookie jar, or on your laptop screen? Everywhere you go. At different times of the day. When you wake up, and when you go to bed. Remind yourself of what your Father said.

"Above all else, guard your heart."

Let's tend to the soil of your heart. Ask the Father to reveal any debris preventing His Word from taking root in your heart. Is there past pain trying to get you to doubt the goodness of God and His will for you to be in health and prosper in every area of your life? Are there disappointments you haven't quite dealt with or processed with Him?

As He reveals the rocks and thorns, allow Him to gently remove them. Just surrender to Him. Listen to His voice as He tenderly speaks to you about every situation where faith has been stunted. Let Him breathe new life into every promise planted in your heart.

It's alright if you don't hear Him speak, just trust that He is present with you. And He is gently removing everything holding back your harvest.

"Keep your mouth free of perversity."

What have you been saying about your situation? Are *your* words in alignment with the word God gave you for this circumstance? Perversity is not just profanity. It is anything in opposition to the life and light contained in those incorruptible seeds you planted in your heart.

Life and death are in the power of your tongue. (See Proverbs 18:21). There will be times when you feel tempted to speak words of hopelessness and discouragement. In those moments, it is important to run to the Father and speak to Him. Let Him remind you of His grace and kindness. He is not going to let His word fail (see Isaiah 55:11). In fact, let me remind you what it says in Luke 1:37 from the Amplified Classic:

> *"For with God nothing is ever impossible and no word from God shall be without power or impossible of fulfillment."*

The power of your breakthrough is contained within the Word. Keep your words in alignment with His words. Do not come into agreement with death. Be ready with the truth when the doubt begins to tap you on the shoulder. Send it away with the authority the Father has bestowed upon you.

"Let your eyes look straight ahead; fix your gaze directly before you."

Vision is vital. The Bible tells us without vision we perish (See Proverbs 29:18). Can you see the promise before it manifests? Can you praise God for your breakthrough, even before it happens?

It can be tempting to 'be realistic' and 'do the math' and look at the 'logical perspective'. But we do not rule and reign from this realm. We are seated, in Christ, in heavenly places. (See Ephesians 2:6). It's Heaven's logic that applies to us.

I'm reminded of Mary, who wrote her beautiful song of praise, thanking God for the Salvation he was bringing through her baby who was not yet born. In this song, she describes in detail what Salvation looks like. (See Luke 1:49-55).

What will Salvation look like for you? Write it down in detail. Write a song of praise. Start every day thanking God for what He is doing in you, through you, and for you. Fix your eyes on Him.

"Give careful thought to the paths for your feet and be steadfast in all your ways."

When we're going through a trial, it can often feel like the ground is shaking beneath us. There will be times when you feel strong, standing firm in your faith. When you're surrounded by people of faith, it is easier to remain standing.

Was this perhaps the reason why Mary took herself away from her home environment for the first three months after she received the Word from Gabriel?

She spent time with her cousin Elizabeth, who was a sign and wonder herself; the evidence of what is possible when God makes a promise to you.

Pay attention to where you go and who you share your heart with, especially in the early days of receiving a promise. Don't let the unbelief of others make you doubt what God has said to you. There will always be people who will want you to look at things from a natural perspective, but you, dear friend, belong to a Kingdom that cannot be shaken. (See Hebrews 12:28).

Ask the Father to help you navigate any tricky relationships. Allow Him to show you where you need to be careful and how to steer your conversations away from doubt. He is faithful, He is with you, and He will lead you perfectly.

CAN I PRAY FOR YOU?

Heavenly Father,

I thank you for the person reading this book. You know them by name. You know the number of hairs on their head. They are worth more to you than many sparrows. I pray they will have ears to hear the promises you speak over their lives. May they have tender hearts to receive the incorruptible seed of your Word. Give them eyes to see the wonderful, abundant life you offer them. Surround them with people who will encourage them to reach for every perfect gift you have prepared for them. May they be rooted and grounded in your love. May they carry Salvation into every circumstance of life-not just for themselves, but for the world around them.

In Jesus Name, Amen.

YOU ARE DEEPLY LOVED.

The Father cares deeply about you. You are constantly on His mind. He doesn't miss any detail of your life. It is His love that activates and energises our faith. (See Galatians 5:6 specifically in the Amplified Classic).

It is the revelation of the Father's love that transformed my life and banished doubt from my heart. I share about this encounter in my book, Untangled.

Once I understood how the Father felt about me, the walls I built around my heart came crashing down. I realised God was not disappointed in me. He was not tired of my struggle or frustrated with my inability to get it right. He was moved with compassion for me, and His desire for me was to be free.

"It is for freedom that Christ has set us free. Stand firm, then, and do not let yourselves be burdened again by a yoke of slavery." (Galatians 5:1, NIV)

I started to learn how to hear His voice, and more importantly, how to discern His voice from the voice of the enemy. It started my process of becoming untangled from every lie that has kept me stuck.

To get untangled we need to hear the words of the Father spoken over our hearts.

The Father wants you to experience the freedom you were created for. If you would like to learn more about getting untangled, you are invited to visit my website, where you will be able to download a copy of the Heart Prints eBook. In this eBook, you will find 10 Words from the Father, that were written down with you in mind.

I also have a selection of Reading Plans on the YouVersion Bible App. These are based on my book, Untangled: Get Untangled The Empowering Love of the Father

If you would like to share your thoughts, you are welcome to send me an email: meliza@melizafarndell.com

About the Author

Meliza Farndell is an accomplished author and the director of Paper Crown Media Ltd. With a deep passion for empowering individuals to break free from limiting beliefs, Meliza guides people in discovering their true identity and purpose. She has a special heart for helping women recognize their infinite worth through the lens of their Heavenly Father.

Meliza's literary work spans both non-fiction and children's books, where she shares the profound, transformative love of God. Proud of her South African heritage, she currently resides in the United Kingdom with her husband and two teenagers.

Connect with Meliza at www.melizafarndell.com or reach out via email at meliza@melizafarndell.com.

Chapter Two

Launched into Destiny

Shirley Chancellor

"If you know that God loves you, you should never question a directive from Him. It will always be right and best. When He gives you a directive, you are not just to observe it, discuss it, or debate it. You are to obey it."

Henry Blackaby

MY SISTER USED TO laugh heartily whenever she shared with others my crude description of our upbringing. I had told her, "We weren't raised, we were yanked up by the hair of the head." She thought that was hilarious, but she agreed this statement was the perfect depiction of our childhood. In truth—we never had one. As hard as things were, I don't regret a single experience of those days. My life is now a testimony to share and, hopefully, encourage others who are struggling to overcome traumas of the past.

You, too, my friend, will learn to look back and use your life experiences to overcome whatever scars were left behind. Not only that, but you will use them to help others with similar histories to shake free from the debilitating emotional rollercoaster and move on to their destiny, as God originally planned. You are strong and determined to change the course of history for yourself, your family, and others whom God brings into your life. How do I know this about you? You are reading this book, which tells me you are searching for ways to deactivate the triggers sending you into a frenzy of uncontrollable emotions, causing pain and hurt for you and those around you. I also know because I was in the same position for many, many years—a vicious cycle of pain, regret, remorse, repentance, and repeating the cycle over and over again. Yeah, been there—done that!

One thing from that early season followed me throughout most of my life: the spirit of rejection. This caused such a lack of confidence, which stunted my ability to step out at the prompting of the Holy Spirit to do the things the Father was expecting me to do. It is a dangerous thing to ignore the Father's direction or assignment. Just ask Jonah—he ended up in the belly of a whale!

> *"The LORD gave this message to Jonah, son of Amittai: "Get up and go to the great city of Nineveh. Announce my judgment against it because I have seen how wicked its people are." But Jonah got up and went in the opposite direction to get away from the LORD. He went down to the port of Joppa, where he found a ship leaving for Tarshish. He bought a ticket and went on board, hoping to escape from the LORD by sailing to Tarshish. Now the LORD had arranged for a great fish to swallow Jonah. And Jonah was inside the fish for three days and three nights."*
>
> Jonah 1:1-3 & 17, NLT

It took years to understand I had a loving Father who cared about every aspect of my life and who had never rejected me and never would.

> *"In the place where they were told, 'You are nobody,' this will be the very place where they will be renamed 'Children of the living God.'"*
>
> Romans 9:26, TPT

You Love Me How Much, Lord???

The Father loves fairly and equally. However, He had a really hard time convincing me. I was a real tough nut to crack, but He never gave up on me. A tremendous breakthrough for me came one day as I was reading the book of John. In chapter 17, Jesus had gone to the garden of Gethsemane to pray. I read as He prayed for His disciples, asking the Father to protect them, to help them remain united, and to guard their hearts against evil. But as I read further, I realized He was also praying for *me and you*. In verse 20, He begins to pray for those in the future who would one day believe because of His disciples' teachings. The part which completely changed my life was when I read how God loves us, <u>just as He loves Jesus</u>. What???? I just sat there and read this verse over and over. It shocked me to realize God loves us, *you and me*, with the SAME passionate love He has for His Son. It is almost beyond our ability to comprehend. Look for yourself:

> *"And I ask not only for these disciples, but also for all those who will one day believe in me through their message. I pray for them all to be joined together as one even as you and I, Father, are joined together as one. I pray for them to become one with us so that the world will recognize that you sent me. For the very glory you have given to me, I have given them so that they will be joined together as one and experience the same unity that we enjoy. You live fully in me and now I live fully in them so that they will experience perfect unity, and the world will be convinced that you have sent me, for they will see <u>that you love each one of them with the same passionate love that you have for me.</u>"*
>
> John 17:20-23, TPT

He repeats it in verse 26. This absolutely wrecked me. I began to weep and cry out to Him, asking for forgiveness and thanking Him for showing me a Father's love. It was something I had longed for and yearned for all my life. I had an amazing encounter with our Lord right then and there. Not once since then have I felt unloved or unwanted. I had security and a promise of eternal love and fellowship with my Lord. This life no longer held any real value for me except for the fact I still had a destiny to fulfill.

You and I are not orphans, half-brothers, half-sisters, or any other negative label or term people care to add to indicate less than being whole. I know this because, as believers, we are covered by the blood of the Lamb. Never let anyone make you feel differently. He lives in us! John 4:13 says He is in us and we are in Him. Also, our Lord assures us in His word He considers all of His children equal. In essence, we carry His DNA!

> *"Even for us, whether we are Jews or non-Jews, we are those he has called to experience his glory. Remember the prophecy God gave in Hosea: "To those who were rejected and not my people, I will say to them: 'You are mine.' And to those who were unloved, I will say: 'You are my darling.'" And: "In the place where they were told, 'You are nobody,' this will be the very place where they will be renamed 'Children of the living God.'"*
>
> Romans 9:24-26, TPT

Wow—Wow—Wow! Doesn't that just break down all kinds of walls we have put up to protect ourselves from the feeling of not belonging or being unwanted? It doesn't matter what has been said to us or what has been done to us. The ones perpetrating evil on us will have to answer for it one day, and it is not our concern, nor is it any of our business how or when it happens. They belong to God just as we do, and He will judge, not us. When you can grasp this and let go of the resentment or whatever feelings you have blocking a truly amazing encounter with Jesus, you will be amazed at how He will interact with you. The encounter I will share below is just one of many occurring after I accepted His love and let go of being led by my feelings and emotions. You have so much to look forward to, precious one.

There is truly no discrimination or favoritism in our Father's heart. I'm not sure about you, but I thought for a long time God only loved the Jews. I was so wrong. Consider the example of Peter's vision in Acts, chapter 10. Peter sees a large sheet descending from above holding many kinds of animals, reptiles, and wild birds. The Jewish people were always forbidden to eat any of those things. However, a voice said to him, "Nothing is unclean if God declares it to be clean." The vision was repeated three times. In the meantime, three men sent by Cornelius, a Roman military captain, were on their way to get Peter to take him to Cornelius' home. Peter had been told in advance by the Spirit to go with them. Once there, he reminded them it was unlawful for him to associate with or even visit the home of anyone who was not a Jew. However, he explained what the Lord had just shown him—he should never look at anyone as inferior or ritually unclean.

This was quite a revelation, but even more so as I studied the Old Testament, which is under the Old Covenant. I saw examples of God accepting people who were not Israelites even way back then—long before Christ was sent to be born of a virgin. One well-known example in Exodus 18 is Moses' father-in-law, Jethro. Although he was a Midianite, Jethro gained respect and served as an advisor for Moses. Another found in Joshua 2 is the harlot, Rahab, who protected the spies in Jericho. The Israelites spared her and her family and later allowed them to live among them in the promised land. She is also listed in the genealogy of Christ in Matthew 1:5.

In the book of Ruth, we learn Ruth was a Moabite who married an Israelite. She learned about God and came to love His people as her own. After her first husband's death, she returned with her mother-in-law to Judah, where she met and married Boaz. She was highly favored by God, so much so an entire book of the bible is devoted to her story.

I had such a deep-rooted belief I did not belong anywhere or to anyone, so I desperately searched the scriptures for proof we were all accepted equally and loved equally by our Father. I was not disappointed.

Is This Really You, Lord?

When you are just learning to hear the voice of the Lord, you tend to doubt whether what you are hearing is truly from Him. I was so afraid I would do the opposite of His will. I would ask for all kinds of signs to make sure it was His voice speaking and not just my imagination or my own desires to do or accomplish something.

I heard Bill Johnson say in a sermon one day, "Delayed obedience *is* disobedience." Wow, did I ever learn this principle the hard way! An encounter one day with the Lord set me straight on the dangers of delaying obedience once and for all. I didn't think of it as disobeying. I was trying to make sure I heard Him right, or if what I was hearing was truly from Him. Now I realize I was just making excuses to avoid doing what He asked.

I was a newly ordained pastor. Our church had been closed for quite some time because of our pastor's long illness and subsequent passing. I loved our community, but it had been dying spiritually for years. Church attendance was down in most area churches, and few of them had any young people left at all. There was a dark cloud over our entire area and I had been praying about it for quite a while. So, God led me to re-open the church, and if nothing else, use it as a home base for an online ministry. I started a social media page for our church, and with the help of our former associate pastor, upgraded the website I had created for our congregation a couple of years earlier.

The Lord was nudging me to start a women's prayer warrior group and book study, but I just didn't have a clue where to begin. The desire was to connect women from different churches in our area so we could bind together in prayer for the needs of our community. As I shared earlier, I would think about it, imagine how and when it would begin, where, who to invite, and how to approach others about being a part of it, etc. Every time I started to do an online invitation to get started, I would have thoughts of how unworthy and ill-prepared I was to be teaching others the Word of God or leading others. I was terrified. I had spent several weeks agonizing about it and knew the Lord was prompting me to begin.

However, things came to a head one morning when I got another word from Him.

This time He said clearly, almost audibly, "If you don't do what the Father has asked you to do, He is going to give your assignment to someone else." Boom! This was the most terrifying message of all! I felt like one of those people we read about in the Old Testament when a high priest would come to them to deliver a stern warning from God about what they would lose because of their disobedience. Some examples below popped into my head:

Saul was no longer allowed to be the king of Israel.

> *Samuel replied to Saul, "I will not return with you. Because you rejected the word of the Lord, the Lord has rejected you from being king over Israel."*
>
> I Samuel 15:26, CSB

Neither Moses nor Aaron were allowed to go into the promised land.

> *"For both of you broke faith with me among the Israelites at the Waters of Meribath-kadesh in the Wilderness of Zin by failing to treat me as holy in their presence. Although from a distance you will view the land that I am giving the Israelites, you will not go there."*
>
> Deuteronomy 32:51-52, CSB

The Israelites were forced to wander in the wilderness until all who had disobeyed passed away. Only Jacob and Caleb were allowed to enter along with those who were under the age of 20 at the time of their exodus from Egypt.

> *"You will bear the consequences of your iniquities forty years based on the number of the forty days that you scouted the land, a year for each*

> *day. You will know my displeasure. I, the Lord, have spoken. I swear that I will do this to the entire evil community that has conspired against me. They will come to an end in the wilderness, and there they will die."*
>
> Numbers 14:34-35, CSB

You can see why I felt the seriousness of this final warning and finally stepped out to do as I was told. We cannot ignore the prompting of the Spirit for any reason or at any time. If it is weighing heavily on your heart to do something for the Lord, it is the Holy Spirit convicting you, and it is wise to follow through.

So even though I was still terrified after the last stern warning, I swallowed my pride and fought down the fear. I made a video to post on social media about the prayer warrior group and book study I wanted to start in our area. Did you notice that? I was afraid, but I did it anyway! A couple of other ladies stepped up to help spread the word, and our journey began and is still going. We have grown so much together and have learned more about our Father along the way. The Lord has taught me a great deal as I reach out to disciple others, and He continues to disciple me as well.

This experience also launched my ministry. The book/bible studies continued for over five years. The prayer warrior group continues to this day, but my ministry has grown as well. I am not only a full-time pastor at a local church, but we have an online ministry as well. We are a small congregation, so our outreach is to sow into other ministries, evangelists, and some who help our local community.

> *"There will be no peace in any soul until it is willing to obey the voice of God."*
>
> D.L. Moody

This quote has proven so very true for me. You can tell the agony and indecisiveness in my wrestling with the Lord in the passages above. Have you been there? Are you getting a nudge to do something or help with something, and you're just not sure what to do? Or do you strive with feeling unworthy, ill-equipped, or worry about what others may think? Please, precious one, do not wait until you are severely chastised by the Holy Spirit as I was. In truth, we *do* know if it is something the Lord is putting in our spirit.

When we are being prompted to do something and feel convicted about it, then it is not the Lord's desire. We are convicted if it is against His will. I wasn't convicted; I was scared and thinking of every excuse in the book not to follow through with what I knew I was to do.

In the Bible, conviction is often associated with the work of the Holy Spirit, who convicts people of their sin and guilt before God. According to John 16:8, the Holy Spirit will convict the world of sin, righteousness, and judgment.

> *"When he comes, he will convict the world about sin, righteousness, and judgment."*
>
> John 16:8, CSB

I was not walking in sin, I was striving to follow Christ, and living a life more righteous than I ever have. If you are living in sin, you're living with constant conviction. I'm going to great lengths to explain the difference because it is important to know if you're being convicted or being prompted to move out and work to help expand the Kingdom. I was already at peace with God as far as my lifestyle goes, but I was just not at peace in understanding what to do from there and was uncomfortable with the assignment before me.

OBEDIENCE AND SURRENDER DEEPEN OUR RELATIONSHIP WITH HIM

My encounter with the Holy Spirit was terrifying but at the same time so encouraging because I came to understand how much He trusted me to fulfill His plans. He had no doubt I could do what He was asking; He was just losing patience with my refusal to "get on with it."

Are you delaying the call on your life? Take some time to really think about it. Are you being led into some kind of ministry or service? If so, don't waste time analyzing it and trying to figure out how, where, finances, etc. If He is asking you to do it, He will provide all you need to carry it out.

Are you wrestling with the feeling you need to be doing more?

Have you had thoughts of reaching out to accomplish something but just weren't sure you were supposed to?

Does the same idea or desire to move out into a new season keep penetrating your mind over and over?

More than likely, the Lord is prompting you to change course, begin to fulfill your destiny, or simply help someone in need. There could be so many more possibilities, but the point is if you are having recurring thoughts as described in the list above, you are being prompted to move into His will. It may take prayer and fasting for you to fully understand what you are being led to do, but the outcome is so worth it.

Earlier in this chapter, I explained how very much the Father loves each one of us. For me, and I'll bet for you also, understanding this changes everything. Believing this builds faith, courage, and determination. Read those scriptures again where Christ prays for us and tells the Father that He understands we are all loved just as He is. Surrendering and receiving His love drives fear away and gives you the resolve to do everything in your power to serve and obey Him. You can and will walk into your destiny. You are so loved and trusted to help advance His Kingdom. Me and the Lord know you can do it!

I did not want to do what He was asking. I fought it, not because I did not want to serve Him, but because I felt so unworthy to do what He was asking. It was hard to believe He would trust me to do something in our community that big. It really wasn't, but to me, it felt tremendous. The Holy Spirit had to use a little "tough love" in my situation. Hopefully, you won't be as hesitant as I was.

Just as the subheading of this section says, obedience and surrender deepen our relationship with Him. When I gave in and started the outreach, just as He was leading me to do, I felt closer to Him than ever before. I felt His love wash over me—I still do! My prayer life became a close walk and fellowship with Him. I was confident to go to Him for help.

To prove that point, I had no finances to speak of for additional ministry. However, miraculously, the money was always there when the time came to buy more books for our studies. I was determined the church would cover the cost because I did not want anyone to feel I was charging for their participation in our endeavor to work together and bring peace and deliverance to our area. Donations began to come from unexpected places. Sometimes I was just overwhelmed by the miracle of it all.

It was not only for this one outreach but also for our church. We were just a handful at the time, with very little finances. Miracles happened often, but one particular time I'd like to share with you is when we needed some updates and repairs to our building. It was going to be a little over $1,000. It may as well have been a million. I did not have it, but I wasn't worried. I walked into the sanctuary one day and fell on my face before the Lord and told Him what we needed. The building belonged to Him. He had paid for it, literally (a story for another time). I prayed, "Father, this is *your* building. You are trusting me to take care of it, but I need help." I told Him how much was needed (as if He didn't know), and I thanked Him in advance for providing it.

I had no idea *how* it would happen, but our relationship had deepened to the point I just knew He would provide. He always had and always would. Listen closely—by the end of that very day, I received $500 from someone who did not and had never attended our church. They said the Lord had laid it on their heart to send it to me. I was sobbing at that, but it didn't end there. By the end of that *very* week, I had over $1,000 and could take care of the needed repairs. And catch this...not one penny of it was from current members of our ministry. They would have if they could, but we were already doing all we could.

Obedience and surrender deepen your relationship. Never forget that. Constant communication with the Lord, listening and following, obeying and worshiping, and setting aside time to draw nearer to Him brings peace and joy most of us have never known before.

I am so eternally grateful the Lord did not give up on me. I have witnessed so many miracles and healings, seen angels, had open visions, prophetic dreams, and witnessed deliverances. Even though I had to be launched into my destiny instead of walking gracefully and obediently as I should have, I am so thankful for that push.

I am so excited for you, my friend. Don't be afraid to listen closely to that still, small voice. It is the voice of the Holy Spirit urging you to move out of your comfort zone and into the destiny the Lord planned for you before the foundations of the world.

> *"For he chose us in him, before the foundation of the world, to be holy and blameless in love before him. He predestined us to be adopted as sons through Jesus Christ for himself, according to the good pleasure of his will, to the praise of his glorious grace that he lavished on us in the Beloved One."*
>
> Ephesians 1:4-6, CSB

> *"For I know the plans I have for you"-this is the LORD's declaration-"plans for your well-being, not for disaster, to give you a future and a hope."* (Jeremiah 29:11, CSB)
>
> Jeremiah 29:11, CSB

MY PRAYER FOR YOU

Father, I ask for wisdom and understanding to flow for this beloved child of yours. Help them hear you clearly and to readily distinguish your voice from the many voices flooding our thoughts each day. Give them clarity and direction, leading to your will for their lives. I pray for peace and harmony in all relationships for them. Father, protect them and their families as they step out in faith to fulfill the destiny you planned for them. Let them flow in the gifts as well as the fruits of your Spirit. I ask all these things in the mighty name of Jesus Christ, our King. Amen.

About the Author

Shirley Chancellor is a retired educator who is now serving in her small community of Bismarck, Arkansas, as the pastor of Light House Christian Church. She hosts a weekly podcast called *At the Table with Shirley*. She loves to read, write, garden, crochet, and most of all, spend time with her family. Shirley is a mother, grandmother, and recently a great-grandmother. Her passion is to share her life-transforming story and usher others into a life of peace and freedom.

Shirley is also a recently published author. Her book, *Deactivation Triggers: Finding Joy and Peace in the Middle of a Chaotic, Angry World,* can be found at amazon.com in print, ebook, and audio format.

If you would like to know more about the author, you can find additional information on the following links:

Website: www.shirleychancellor.com
Facebook: @shirleychancellor2020
Instagram: @shirleychancellorministries

Chapter Three

Embraced by Love

Andrea John

Engulfed in darkness, I sat on the cold tile floor, sobbing in disbelief at the words that had just escaped my mouth—words as shocking to me as they were to my mom and, I imagined, to God. How broken had I become? I didn't recognize myself. With my head in my hands, I kept thinking, "Who am I?"

The shattered phone before me mirrored the broken fragments of my life. My entire being had split into a thousand shards, and I had no idea how to piece them back together. Even if I could, would it work? What if this was it? Was I now broken for life—lost, alone, and hopeless?

Have you ever felt this way?

It wasn't just about the actual phone; it was just a physical representation of the internal chaos with which I had been struggling. I had been walking in the dark without realizing it. At some point, your eyes adjust, and you believe you see clearly, but in reality, you're navigating a room, using all your senses to get through it. Everything becomes difficult, even the simplest of tasks.

It's hard to pinpoint when I entered the darkness. It wasn't a sudden plunge but a gradual dimming of light. Perhaps a dim light eventually burned out, or I turned away from it, walking deeper into darkness until I was engulfed by all its friends-confusion, anger, bitterness, chaos, hatred, loneliness, and hopelessness.

Imagine standing in a room where the lights gradually dim until you can no longer distinguish familiar objects. The darkness becomes more than the absence of light; it becomes a tangible force, a shroud wrapping around your soul.

Confusion is a constant in this dimly lit existence, whispering doubts and distorting perceptions. Anger and bitterness intertwine, covering you in a tapestry of despair. Chaos reigns, turning even the simplest moments into complicated puzzles, filled with hatred, leaving a lingering bitter aftertaste.

Loneliness is an echo in the dark, a companion walking beside you even in a crowded room. Hopelessness, a heavy weight on your shoulders, makes every step a struggle. It's not just darkness; it's a realm where the very essence of your being is unclear.

It's accompanied by an isolation that causes you to think you are the only one who feels this way; the experience is unique to you. I have learned walking in the darkness is not uncommon, and some may relate to every word I just described. Maybe that's you.

I had been living a broken life for a couple of years. As a mother of two beautiful girls, I couldn't afford to break down completely. I wore the facade of "being okay," yet within, the pieces frivolously clung together, desperately trying to hang on but capable of falling apart at any moment. It felt like I was living in a glass house, fragile and vulnerable to destruction.

Living this shattered existence meant waking up each day with a weight pressing on my chest, making it hard to breathe. Simple tasks became monumental challenges, and laughter felt like a distant memory.

I carried this brokenness in the quiet moments when everyone thought I had it all together. It was a silent struggle, the invisible fractures beneath a carefully crafted appearance. The broken pieces within me weren't just fragments; they were the echoes of a battle waged silently, where no longer could the strongest facade conceal the internal chaos.

Shattered Pieces

Thankfully, I was surrounded by people who loved me through it. Their unwavering support became my lifeline, a light breaking through the unending darkness. Yet, despite being surrounded by love, I felt profoundly alone, trapped in an isolation only I could understand.

Amid all the despair, my mom was an incredible source of support. She would spend hours on the phone listening to me vent, cry, get frustrated, and sometimes talk about the silliest things to help pass the time. One day, as usual, I was on the phone with her venting about a legal situation I was going through, and she said, "It's going to be okay. God is working it out." A seemingly harmless statement meant to comfort me.

The shards of broken pieces within me came tumbling down, creating an explosion within. I pulled the phone's mouthpiece closer to my lips and yelled, "I don't even know if I believe God exists anymore!" The next thing I knew, I pulled my arm back, threw the phone across the room, hitting a wall, and watched the phone turn into tiny pieces gliding across the floor. I fell to my knees in absolute despair, engulfed in darkness. *How could I say what I did?* This was the moment I realized just how dark everything was around me.

Hearing those words was monumentally devastating, and now, not only was I broken, but I had just broken my mom's heart and, perhaps, even God's.

Faith in God has been embedded in my core since childhood. I could not imagine a world without Him. Yet, in that moment, I uttered words that seemed to shake through the heavens, causing a fracture in the foundation of my faith and my entire being.

I imagined God, who had been there through every joy and sorrow, looking at me with tears in His eyes and heart heavy with sadness. It was as if the universe paused, holding its breath in response to my declaration. The pain in God's eyes mirrored the brokenness within me.

In those moments of doubt, I sensed God's heartbreak, a tear in the connection that had been an anchor throughout my life. It wasn't just about my struggle, but about disappointing the essence of who I was. It was about unintentionally challenging unconditional love. Here I sat alone, tears streaming down my face, surrounded by the suffocating embrace of darkness and all the shattered pieces of who I once was. How could I put myself back together if I no longer knew who I was?

God Put the Pieces Back Together

Life doesn't stop when we are in an existential crisis. The world carries on, no matter how broken we are. As a mom of two precious daughters, I didn't have the luxury of time to figure out how to put all the pieces together. So, as I did with the shattered phone, I swept everything up and threw it away in the trash. I'd been walking around as a shell of my former self for such a long time. I successfully built a strong facade, so the plan was to power through for my girls, hoping it would all work out in the end. Have you ever been at a point where you felt lost but didn't have the time to figure out the directions because you had to take care of others?

Thankfully, I had a mother who gathered an army of people from around the world to pray for me. The encounter I am about to share was influenced by the prayers of my mother, family, and all those seeking God on my behalf. While drowning in the pit of despair, God was listening to and answering the prayers of all those approaching His throne praying for me.

My shattered heart and my mind tangled in dark thoughts didn't create a space allowing me to meet God. For months, I couldn't pray or read the Bible. Why would God want anything to do with me? My life was in shambles, and my doubts were like massive clouds blocking the sun's light. I was sure God wouldn't have space to speak to me because I thought He'd have nothing good to say.

What I didn't realize was that God would go to great lengths to pursue me. He knew my heart and knew what I needed—love that casts out fear.

Just a few weeks later, I began my day as always. My mornings were predictable even then.

Before heading to my home office, I turned on the coffeemaker. The smell of coffee filled the air as I booted up my computer to begin my workday. It had been a few months since I had been on Facebook, and I had decided to rejoin the social media world—at least to see what was going on.

The first post I saw was my dad sharing a video of my sister-in-law leading a worship song at her church called "At the Cross." My coffee machine began beeping, letting me know my caffeine fix was ready, so I decided to click play, turn up the speakers, and start making my breakfast. I would make the same thing I had every morning: eggs, sautéed veggies, and Ezekiel toast. My cast iron pan was already on the stove, so I turned on the burner, allowing the pan to warm up while I pulled out all my ingredients.

The song filling the house was familiar, and the guy singing had a phenomenal voice, to no surprise. As I was about to crack the eggs, my sister-in-law sang the second verse, saying, "And there's a place where sin and shame are powerless. Where my heart has peace with God and forgiveness. Where all the love I've ever found comes like a flood. Comes flowing down…"

The moment her angelic voice filled my kitchen, I felt God's overwhelming, gracious presence. It felt like my body was melting, and I dropped to my knees as tears streamed down my face, the love of God embracing me like a big, heavy blanket. Have you ever had a warm, heavy blanket over you? Doesn't it feel so comforting? That's what it felt like, but better. Honestly, there are no words to describe this transcendent moment. Any possible words I could use to describe this encounter will fall short.

In that moment, God lifted every burden, calmed my nerves, and set me free from the fear ruling over me my entire life. Faintly in the background, I could hear the voices of the people praying for me, and in response, God said to me, "Andrea, I've been here all along."

It's hard to say how long I was on the floor, embraced by Love that morning. Mere moments felt like days. There wasn't a conversation with God, and other than God telling me He was with me all along, no other audible words were spoken. Those enlightening moments flooded my heart with wisdom and understanding of God's love. It was a knowing; revelation. I could feel, sense, and see the depths of who God is as love.

God wasn't disgusted with me and didn't condemn me. He didn't ask me how I didn't know better or call me out on my doubts. He simply and beautifully showered me with His love, revealing the truth about His nature's essence as Scripture described when John shared, "God is love."

God is love. He doesn't just love. He *is* love. Who He is, and everything He does is from His love. That is why nothing can separate us from the love of God, as Paul wrote in Romans 8:35, 38-39 (NRSV):

> *Who will separate us from the love of Christ? Will hardship, or distress, or persecution, or famine, or nakedness, or peril, or sword?...For I am convinced that neither death, nor life, nor angels, nor rulers, nor things present, nor things to come, nor powers, nor height, nor depth, nor anything else in all creation, will be able to separate us from the love of God in Christ Jesus our Lord.*

In addition to God answering the prayers of every living person who had been praying for me, I also experienced the response to one of Apostle Paul's prayers.

> *When I think of the wisdom and scope of his plan, I fall down on my knees and pray to the Father of all the great family of God—some*

of them already in heaven and some down here on earth—that out of his glorious, unlimited resources he will give you the mighty inner strengthening of his Holy Spirit. And I pray that Christ will be more and more at home in your hearts, living within you as you trust in him. May your roots go down deep into the soil of God's marvelous love; and may you be able to feel and understand, as all God's children should, how long, how wide, how deep, and how high his love really is; and to experience this love for yourselves, though it is so great that you will never see the end of it or fully know or understand it. And so at last you will be filled up with God himself.
                                           Ephesians 3:14-19, TLB

God, the One who is Love, came into my kitchen that morning, and it felt like the first time I had ever met Him.

Growing up in the church, I was no casual attendee. From an early age, I actively participated in several weekly church activities, deeply involved in many areas. Yet, that intimate encounter with God revealed a sad truth—I didn't know God. I thought God would want nothing to do with me because of my anger, bitterness, and inadequacy, but the opposite happened. God took me into His arms and loved me back to life.

When I rose from the floor, I felt a profound transformation coursing through me. The external conflicts and circumstances which had destroyed me remained unchanged. Yet, an extraordinary shift happened within me, and I suddenly knew who I was. I was His. I was His daughter made in His image and likeness.

His grace rewired my very being, rendering everything different. The broken pieces of my life no longer seemed impossible to put back together because the picture of who I was created to be was revealed to me. The picture was not of me but of God, the One who is love.

I was lost and broken for the longest time, unsure of who I was. Can you relate? That morning, I realized I had been looking in the wrong places. Since I had seen

God and experienced Him, I knew who I was. I was formed and created to bear God's image and likeness.

God revealed so much to me that morning. Here are two keys that have become the core of who I am, and driving what I do: Key #1–Love, and Key #2–Made in the Image of God.

These keys have become the core of who I am and drive what I do. They have allowed me to experience the fullness of life in God and the promises of Jesus; peace that makes no sense to the human mind (Philippians 4:6-7), joy that words cannot explain (1 Peter 1:8), and love that banishes fear (1 John 4:18).

I want you to experience this life, so I'd love to share these two keys.

KEY #1—LOVE

As God embraced me, the Scripture "God is love" came alive.

> "God is love, and all who live in love live in God, and God lives in them."
>
> 1 John 4:16b, NLT

I met Love. Not love the verb; Love the person. What an incredible meeting it was.

In all my years attending church and serving God, the infamous passage of 1 Corinthians 13 never felt real to me. It seemed impossible for someone to love that way. And if I'm honest, I didn't even believe God could love me in that way. I believed in the Bible, but *not that part*. All this changed when I met Love.

> "Love is patient and kind. Love is not jealous or boastful or proud or rude. It does not demand its own way. It is not irritable, and it keeps no record of being wronged. It does not rejoice about injustice but

> *rejoices whenever the truth wins out. Love never gives up, never loses faith, is always hopeful, and endures through every circumstance."*
>
> 1 Corinthians 13:4-7, NLT

I knew a great deal about what God did, but now I wanted to get to know who He was. Meeting Love launched me into a journey of getting to know Him and discovering His true nature. Over the years, when I read Scripture, I always look for what God reveals about Himself in every story and letter.

There's a difference between discussing God and what He does. When we focus on God, His actions in every circumstance become clearer because we know the heart behind them.

God doesn't just love. God is Love. His essence is Love. Every facet of His being radiates love. God exists within love, and love resides within God. God's core is love.

> *"God showed how much he loved us by sending his one and only Son into the world so that we might have eternal life through him. This is real love—not that we loved God, but that he loved us and sent his Son as a sacrifice to take away our sins."*
>
> 1 John 4:9-10, NLT

Genuine love is found in God, the kind every human craves and needs. He is the source of love. Without Him, love is not possible. We love because He first loved us. Those who have experienced true love can never keep it to themselves. They will always find ways to love others as they have been loved because they know how transforming it is.

The beautiful thing about living in love is how it allows us to reflect God on earth. Those who experience your genuine love are experiencing God. They may not realize it, but that's what is happening. Loving someone well can change their life forever.

> *"Dear friends, since God loved us that much, we surely ought to love each other. No one has ever seen God. But if we love each other, God lives in us, and his love is brought to full expression in us."*
>
> 1 John 4:11-12, NLT

To be a child of God, you must love. Living in love reveals you are a child of God because you are made in His image and likeness.

> *"Dear friends, let us continue to love one another, for love comes from God. Anyone who loves is a child of God and knows God. But anyone who does not love does not know God, for God is love."*
>
> 1 John 4:7-8, NLT

As I deepened my relationship with God and explored the pages of Scripture to know Him better, I witnessed a theme emerge from the book of Genesis through to Revelation-Love. God's love for the world and pursuit of a relationship with humanity became clear. We even see it in the popular passage of John 3:16:

> *For God so loved the world that he gave his only Son, so that everyone who believes in him may not perish but may have eternal life.* (NRSVA)

Jesus embodied God's love; through His life, you are empowered to love as He loves. We have all heard the passage where Jesus shares the greatest commandment:

> *"Love the Lord your God with all your heart and with all your soul and with all your mind and with all your strength. The second is this:*

> *'Love your neighbor as yourself. There is no commandment greater than these."*
>
> Mark 12:30-31, NIV

Within the law, loving your neighbor as yourself was a part of the great commandment, but there was a flaw. What would happen on those days when we don't love ourselves very much? The standard of loving others is ourselves, and I don't know about you, but I am not flawless, so how could I be a standard for something so important?

In the Sermon on the Mount, Jesus proclaimed, "I came to fulfill the law, not abolish it" (Matthew 5:17), and in Galatians 5:14, Paul shared how love completes God's laws.

Thankfully, Jesus steps in to become our standard, and this is revealed in the new commandment He left us:

> *"I am giving you a new commandment, that you love one another; just as I have loved you, that you also love one another. By this, all people will know that you are My disciples: if you have love for one another."*
>
> John 13:34-35, NASB

Loving you as I love myself is not always the best reflection of who God is, but loving you like Jesus will never fail to foster an environment infused with God. Loving as Christ loves is a lifelong pursuit, a high calling setting us apart as children of God and disciples of Christ.

Your paramount aim should be to become love as God is love. Love is not just an action; it is who you must become. It is your identity as a child of God and a disciple of Jesus. When you embody love, expressing it becomes natural and effortless. Love is not confined to behavior; it is your essence.

You are created to be love as He is love.

Key #2—Made in the Image of God

Webster's dictionary defines identity as an individual's distinguishing character or personality and the sameness of essential or generic characteristics in different instances. I interpret that as a person's characteristics or attributes that remain the same despite different circumstances.

Identity, according to sociology, is defined a bit differently. It is defined as the qualities, beliefs, personality traits, appearance, and/or expressions that characterize a person or a group. To study sociology, I understand their definition, but I have found so many nowadays have an identity crisis because who they are is based on fleeting and temporary attributes—for example, appearance and even certain personality traits.

While there are personality traits lasting a lifetime, others are more flaws than traits, and defining ourselves by them disturbs the picture of who we should be. I view our personality as a method by which we demonstrate our identity, not our identity itself. The same goes for our appearance. It is a way of expressing our identity but not our identity itself. Tying our identity to potentially temporary expressions, such as personality or appearance, will cause a conflict within ourselves should we ever decide to grow and change.

For this reason, I lean towards the conventional definition of "identity" because it informs us that our identity consists of characteristics that remain the same despite circumstances. Everything we do, what we look like, our personalities, and even differing roles do not impact our identity. Those are all vehicles to showcase our identity.

After my encounter with God that morning, I was suddenly aware of who I was. So many years lost and confused meant nothing now that I had met Love. Without my circumstances changing, it now all made sense because I had experienced God, the One in whose image I was created.

Humanity is uniquely created in God's image, a profound truth we see repeatedly in Scripture. Genesis 1:27 (NIV) declares, *"So God created mankind in his own image, in the image of God he created them; male and female he created them."* This foundational belief provides us with a blueprint of who we were created to be. Our identity, rooted in God's image and likeness, shapes our understanding of ourselves and our relationship with God.

Being made in His image means you are created to reflect God's nature. This includes the capacity for love, creativity, and forming meaningful relationships. Your identity as God's image-bearers is a statement of your worth and a call to live in a way that reflects His character.

Hopefully, understanding this divine design helps you grasp your true identity and reminds you that your mistakes or failures do not define you, but by your Creator. Each person reflects God's image, meticulously designed with purpose and intention. I pray this understanding empowers you to live a life which honors God and demonstrates His love.

Psalms 139 beautifully captures the intimacy and care with which God created us. The psalmist writes, *"For you created my inmost being; you knit me together in my mother's womb. I praise you because I am fearfully and wonderfully made."* (Psalms 139:13-14, NIV). This passage emphasizes how you are intricately and purposefully designed by God, reinforcing your God-given value and purpose in this world.

Your identity as an image-bearer of God calls you to reflect His character. This includes living out love, justice, mercy, and humility. It means recognizing the inherent worth in ourselves and others, as we are all made to look and be like Him.

ACTIVATE LOVE

Spending time with God and meditating on the Scriptures revealing Him has brought the truth into full expression within my life. Two activations may empower you to live out the two keys.

Scripture Meditation: Psalms 139

Take a few moments to meditate on this passage. Close your eyes, take deep breaths, and allow the words to sink into your heart. Reflect on the idea that God makes you fearfully and wonderfully with purpose and intention.

Visualization: Embracing God's Love

Find a quiet and comfortable space where you won't be disturbed. Close your eyes and imagine yourself surrounded by a warm, golden light. This light represents God's love, enveloping you completely. Feel the warmth and comfort of this love washing over you, filling every part of your being with peace and joy.

As you visualize, pray, "God, I open my heart to receive your love. Help me get to know you better and understand who you created me to be. Reveal who I am in your eyes and guide me to live a life that reflects who you are."

Prayer:

As Paul prayed, I pray for you:

> *"I pray that from his glorious, unlimited resources he will empower you with inner strength through his Spirit. Then Christ will make his home in your hearts as you trust in him. Your roots will grow down into God's love and keep you strong. And may you have the power to understand, as all God's people should, how wide, how long, how high, and how deep his love is. May you experience the love of Christ, though it is too great to understand fully. Then you will be made complete with all the fullness of life and power that comes from God."*
>
> Ephesians 3:16-19, NLT

Amen.

ABOUT THE AUTHOR

Andrea John is a devoted wife, mother of two daughters, and a passionate advocate for helping others discover their identity and purpose. Her mission is to empower individuals to live their best lives by embracing their God-given calling. With her husband, Andrea co-leads *Jesus House*, a ministry that focuses on faith, identity, and living in alignment with God's plan.

As the host of the podcast *Destiny Awaits*, Andrea inspires listeners to step into their unique gifts and pursue their divine purpose. Through personal stories, scriptures, and engaging conversations, she creates a space for transformation and growth. Andrea's upcoming book, *In His Image*, launching on September 26, 2024, reflects her heart for teaching and empowering others to see themselves through the lens of God's love and truth.

Andrea believes that knowing who God is leads to understanding our true identity, a message she carries throughout her work and life. Whether through her writing, ministry, or podcast, she is committed to guiding others towards wholeness and purpose.

Connect with Andrea:
Website: www.andreajohn.com
Facebook: @JourneywithAndreaJohn
Instagram: @thejourneywithandrea
Podcast: Destiny Awaits
YouTube: @andreajohn

Chapter Four

Come Follow Me

Pamela Rice

The Power of Purpose and Authenticity

There's a lot of talk about "purpose" these days. People are on a quest to find their identity and significance, seeking a deeper meaning in life. I understand this need well, realizing there must be more to life than superficial self-indulgence. Growing up in a small town in the Midwest, my curiosity drove me to explore life's mysteries and find my place in the world. This search led me on a wild ride, eventually landing me in the entertainment industry in Hollywood. For several years, I lived a life many only dream about, immersed in the glamour and excitement of the spotlight. However, this journey also revealed the darker sides of fame and fortune, challenging my values and ultimately reshaping my understanding of what truly matters.

I experienced how the rich and famous live behind their guarded gates—often struggling with suspicions and uncertainties, trying to maintain the significance of their manufactured images. Where great power and wealth exist, greed, lust, and exploitation abound. Trespassing into that inner sanctum extracts a heavy admission price. It demands total allegiance to its system of avarice and imperceptibly erodes the truth with fool's gold. The world's playgrounds are enticing and cater to the false illusions of self-aggrandizement. *"What do you benefit if you gain the whole world, but lose your own soul?"* (Mark 8:36, NLT). I had no desire to repeat the painful mistakes of my past.

I often thought I'd get it right next time. Next time, it'll be different. After twenty-eight years of doing things my way, where has it gotten me? Do I want to keep pursuing what I think I want? Or is it time to find out who God is?

I paced around my room. I knew I needed help, and maybe God could help me. What did I have to lose? My life lay in shambles, and I didn't know how to fix it. God showed up in the past with unique moments of revelation, but I never pursued them. Once the problem was solved, I'd return to doing things my way. God faded away. This time was different. In my frustration, I looked up, "OK, God! I want to know if you are real. Are you really who you say you are?" Then I added my conditions: "But I don't want 'Churchianity' or a nice little pat on the head. I don't want to warm a pew somewhere. I have real problems and need real answers—either you've got them, or you don't. Either you are who you say you are, or you're not. I need to know the truth!" Now came the ultimatum, "So, here's the deal, God—I'll give you six months. For six months, I'll take your Word literally to the best of my ability. But I'm telling you—the first time I step out and you're not there, I'll pack my little bags, and I won't bother you anymore. I don't know where I'll go or what I'll do, but I won't bother you anymore."

God must have smiled at this audacious little girl who desperately wanted the truth. I didn't mean to be disrespectful, but I had to be honest. Trite platitudes weren't going to cut it. My gaping wounds were hemorrhaging, and no spiritual Band-Aid would stop them. God didn't seem offended by my challenge. No lightning bolt shot out of heaven to strike me down. If nothing is hidden from God, as the Bible says—he already knows my fears—so why try and hide them? If he created me, I doubt anything I did would surprise him. I hid from myself by reasoning and rationalizing my sin—or plain out denying it—but God knew. Maybe I didn't know how to handle my emotions, but I assumed God did.

Trust, vulnerability, and transparency were all dangerous words for me. But if God's love is unconditional, and if he will never leave me, didn't it make sense I could risk trusting him? Maybe I could be vulnerable within the safety of God's love. "OK, God . . . you want my life? You can have it. It's not very pretty, but it's yours." I had no religious pretense in my relationship with God. My desperation caused me to be brutally honest. If I couldn't be authentic, how could I learn to trust? Without trust, how could I ever love him completely? I had to start somewhere; I took my first step of faith. Without this honest relationship, I wouldn't have had the courage to make the hard choices, take risks, and press into the spiritual conflicts waiting around the corner.

The Bible warns us, *"The night is almost gone; the day of salvation will soon be here. So remove your dark deeds like dirty clothes, and put on the shining armor of right living"* (Romans 13:12, NLT). At first, I had no idea what this meant. Right living? Had I been living wrong all along? I always considered myself a good person, but this passage made me realize I was more compromised than I thought. My values aligned more with the world's values than any Biblical principles.

This realization was a stark wake-up call. The "night" in the scripture symbolizes a time of ignorance, moral ambiguity, and spiritual darkness. As dawn approaches, bringing the "day of salvation," we are urged to shed our old ways—our "dark deeds"—as quickly as we would discard dirty clothes. The shining armor of right living represents a transformation, a call to embrace a life of integrity, honesty, and alignment with God's will.

I began to reflect on my life and actions. Was I genuinely embodying the principles of love, kindness, and humility the Bible espouses? Or was I swept up in the self-centered, materialistic values of the world around me? This introspection revealed the truth: while I might have appeared good on the surface, my heart was far from the righteousness God desires.

Understanding this scripture was about recognizing my flaws and realizing the potential for profound change. It was a call to action, urging me to realign my life with spiritual truths and seek a deeper, more meaningful existence. It challenged me to put on the "shining armor" of right living, to protect my soul, and to guide my actions towards a higher, divine purpose.

The Vineyard Christian Fellowship became the first church that felt like home, and Sundays were a day of joyous celebration. The services were brimming with youthful vitality, creativity, and the powerful presence of God. People from all walks of life, including the entertainment industry, attended. Worshiping together and being taught the Word of God forged eternal bonds and created a beautiful spiritual family. The sweet presence of God descended and brought revitalizing refreshment.

The Daisy, a Christian nightclub where musicians performed in a non-alcoholic environment, was turned into a three-month Vineyard School of Discipleship during the day. Since I told God I'd take his Word literally for six months, I figured I'd better find out what it said.

The pastors taught from their expertise on pivotal books of the Bible. A God I never understood was revealed through the depth of the Word. The more I learned, the more fascinated I became. We were going to the school of the Holy Spirit and learning new life skills from a Biblical perspective.

There were twenty-five to thirty students, and it became an accelerated time of spiritual growth. Senior pastor and Vineyard founder Kenn Gulliksen taught my favorite class, "The Principles of Discipleship."

Kenn, a highly respected and gifted teacher, had a gentle way of unlocking the wisdom of scripture. He made the biblical principles relevant and practical. During one of our classes, Kenn suggested we pray for what God placed on our hearts. He led the prayer and opened it to the rest of the class. One by one, different students prayed, including me.

After Kenn closed in prayer and everyone returned to rustling papers, preparing for the next lesson, Kenn made an unusual comment. "We all have our own way of praying," he said. "I pray like the New American Standard Bible, and Pam prays like the Amplified Bible." Everyone laughed . . . except me.

That comment utterly mortified me, and my face flushed with embarrassment. The Amplified Bible expanded the text and used more words than traditional

Bibles. Still needing repair, my self-esteem took it as a chastisement, and I failed to see the humor in what he intended as a playful comment, which devastated me.

Tears plopped onto the pages as my head hung over my open Bible. The sound hitting the tissue-thin paper resounded so loudly I imagined everyone could hear it. I couldn't look at anyone because I thought they were making fun of me for talking too much in prayer.

Kenn suggested a fifteen-minute break before returning to class. I slipped out the side door to avoid any interactions with the students. I had to decide whether to race home in humiliation or find the courage to return to class. The tears wouldn't stop flowing as I stared at the sky, wondering what to do. A verse came to mind: *"Give thanks in all circumstances, for this is God's will for you in Christ Jesus"* (1 Thessalonians 5:18, NIV)

Give thanks in all circumstances. Really? I wiped the snot dripping from my nose.

"OK, let's see," I half-heartedly lifted my hands and said a feeble prayer, "Praise you, Jesus," then cried even harder.

This is insane, sneered a negative voice inside my head.

I tried again, choking back tears, "Praise you, Jesus."

If anyone saw you out here, they'd think you were a complete idiot, chided that cynical voice in my head. What are you praising God for when you're hurting and have tears running down your face? This is absurd!

I wasn't making much headway in the reasoning department.

"Lord, your Word says to praise you in all things, not necessarily for all things." I tried to refute the negative thoughts. Still fearful of how ridiculous I might look, I tried again. "Praise you, Jesus!" Each declaration of praise became stronger with practice.

Walking back to the classroom, the pain lifted, my tears dried, and I sensed a gentle peace by the time I reached the door. I took my seat with the other students with a renewed sense of relief.

What just happened? Where had the pain come from? Kenn had made an innocuous little comment. Why did it strike such a deep chord inside me? The Bible says God inhabits the praises of his people (Psalm 22:3, KJV). Even as weak as mine were, he honored my effort to praise him amid my humiliation and tears.

The Bible encourages us to *"draw near with a sincere heart in full assurance of faith, having our hearts sprinkled clean from an evil conscience and our bodies washed with pure water"* (Hebrews 10:22, NASB). But how could I draw near to God with a self-centered heart? I didn't believe my conscience was evil, yet it was far from clean after a life of sin.

This scripture invites us into a deeper relationship with God. A "sincere heart" implies authenticity and a genuine desire for connection, free from pretense. "Full assurance of faith" suggests a confident trust in God's promises, believing wholeheartedly in His ability to renew us.

However, my journey to understanding this verse was not straightforward. I struggled with feelings of unworthiness and the weight of my past actions. How could I approach God with a "sincere heart" when my life seemed marred by selfish pursuits? Having my heart "sprinkled clean from an evil conscience" seemed beyond reach. But upon deeper reflection, I realized this cleansing is not something I could achieve on my own. It is a divine act of grace.

Acknowledging my flaws was the first step toward letting God purify my heart. It meant trusting that, despite my imperfections, God's love and grace were sufficient.

Drawing near God meant opening myself to His transformative power and aligning with His will. It was about embracing a journey of continual growth, where each step taken in faith brought me closer to the sincerity described above in Hebrews 10:22. The process was not easy.

As I continued to learn the fundamentals of my new faith, I realized I needed spiritual cleansing in the waters of baptism and had to be "born of water."

My parents had me sprinkled with water when they dedicated me as a baby, but total immersion symbolized the death, burial, and resurrection of Jesus. Being immersed in the water meant choosing to identify—symbolically—with the "death" of Jesus and my former life. The old life is "buried" with Christ and washed away, and my new life emerges in "resurrection" power.

> *"Do you not know that all of us who have been baptized into Christ Jesus were baptized into his death? Therefore, we were buried with him by baptism into death so that, just as Christ was raised from the dead by the glory of the Father, we too might walk in the newness of life. For if we have been united with him in a death like his, we shall certainly be united with him in a resurrection like his."*
>
> Romans 6:3–5, ESV

The Vineyard planned a baptism celebration at Santa Monica's beach. Being baptized in the Pacific Ocean sounded exciting.

My white, gauzy top and pants covered my bikini and the thin gold chain around my size-two waist. When I took off my outer garments to prepare for baptism, I realized my tiny bikini barely covered my body. The gentle persuasion of the Holy Spirit made me uncomfortable with my near nakedness. I never owned a one-piece suit, but I could have used one now. I quickly grabbed my top and covered myself. Modesty had returned to my life.

The sun warmed me as I sat on the beach and sang worship songs under a white canopy of puffy clouds. I marveled at the magnitude of God's handiwork while the breeze danced playfully across the ocean. With my toes dug into the sand, I contemplated the importance of my commitment.

"OK, Lord," I whispered, "I am doing this in obedience to your Word. Today, I will bury my old life and wash it out to sea. If I never stand in front of a camera or do anything in Hollywood again, I will live the life you created for me. Today starts my new life with you."

Two pastors held me firmly on either side and plunged me under the water. I rose to soft praises surrounding me—clean and free.

My friend Doug and I drove to the Santa Monica Pier for coffee before heading home. We ordered from a small stand on the pier. I turned and nearly knocked over a disheveled young boy standing behind me. He looked about twelve.

"I am sorry," I said. The boy didn't move. He stood there and stared at me.

"Are you hungry?"

"Yes," he nodded.

I ordered him a hamburger, fries, and a hot chocolate. We moved to a table, and I said, "What's your name?"

"Ray." We sat with him while he ate.

"What are you doing here, Ray?"

"I ran away from a group home and have a bed under the pier."

The thought of a child sleeping in such vulnerable circumstances shocked me. We tried to figure out what we could do for him. Doug worked all day, and I lived alone, but we couldn't let him stay here.

"There's a Christian crisis house in Hollywood that just opened," Doug said, "I think it's called Centrum. Would you like to go there, Ray?"

"They won't turn me in, will they?" He stiffened at the thought.

"I don't think so, but I know they will help you."

Doug called and let them know we were coming.

I stared out the window of the car as we neared the house. Hollywood resembled desolation row with its crumbling, dilapidated buildings, XXX shops, and the odd assortment of characters wandering the streets.

"The city plans to restore this neighborhood and make it a tourist attraction," Doug said, "Right now, this is where the runaway kids hang out and sleep in the squats."

"Squats?"

"The abandoned buildings waiting to be torn down. There are also a lot of working girls around here."

Right off the main strip of Hollywood Boulevard, on Sycamore Street, stood a once beautiful—now dilapidated—two-story house. Its peeled paint and sagging porch steps suggested years of neglect. We walked into what reminded me of a musty thrift store with mismatched furniture and worn-out rugs. As I took in this strange environment, laughter erupted around the corner. I ventured in and encountered a diverse group seated around a dinner table.

"Welcome!" Tim, the house manager, said. "Come in. Want something to eat?"

"No, thank you. We've already eaten."

I knew little about mission work except for the missionaries who went to Africa or a Third World country. But here, in the heart of Hollywood, existed a new kind of mission field. Despite the rundown conditions, a warm lightness caressed me. I'd never witnessed God reaching out to the needs of people in such a practical way. After bringing Ray to Centrum, I followed up with him, while getting to know the staff.

The house only took men. When women sought help, I volunteered to take them to my apartment. My one-bedroom apartment soon became overrun with two girls in my king-size bed, another on the couch in the den, and me on the couch in my living room. The women stayed at the men's house during the day for Bible studies, meals, and activities.

I began to envision a bigger house for more girls. We could hang chintz curtains and bake bread, and Jesus could heal everyone. But rents were too expensive, and it was only a dream, anyway.

"How are you doing, Pam?" Kleg Seth, the founder of Centrum, asked. "You doing OK? Any problems with the girls?"

"No, so far, so good," I said to the lanky Lutheran pastor, who was looking down at me with his smiling eyes.

"You know you can call me day or night if you need anything." Kleg's dedication inspired me. "I know how difficult this can be. You're doing a great job, and I appreciate your help."

"Thanks, Kleg. How do you do it? You're always so calm. When do you sleep?"

He laughed and shook his well-groomed head of red hair. "It's the grace of God that keeps me going." The man worked tirelessly without complaint. The staff drew strength from his stability.

"Pam, we want to open a women's house, and since you've been working with the women, would you consider being the director?"

"Me?" My mouth dropped open. It's one thing to daydream but another when it becomes a reality.

"Yes, we want to rent a house on the next street over for women."

This meant giving up my apartment and living in the house with the girls. "Can I pray about this?"

I hadn't finished the three-month course at the School of Discipleship. Now, they want me to run a crisis house dealing with at-risk youth, prostitutes, and all the other indigents in need. How crazy is this?

I cornered several of the pastors at school. "What do you think of me being the director of Centrum's new women's home?"

They were supposed to say, "Pam, you are not qualified." Instead, they said, "Pam, you'd be great!"

Inside my head, I cried, "What? I'm too young to die!" This move meant death to my independence and way of life.

I went to my senior pastor, Kenn Gulliksen, for confirmation. I mustered the nerve to ask, "What do you think about me directing the women's house in Hollywood?"

Our eyes locked, and tears welled up. There, peering straight into my soul, were the smiling eyes of Jesus. As impossible as it sounds, the supernatural eyes of Jesus looked directly at me through my pastor.

"Pick up your cross and follow Jesus," he said, drawing from Matthew 16:24–26.

As much as I didn't want to hear those words, I knew Jesus spoke through Kenn. I melted into the chair. This should have been the final confirmation I needed, but I still wavered in my decision.

Every time I tried to pray that weekend, my thoughts distracted me.

"I need to go shopping."

"No, I'll go swimming."

My mind couldn't focus. When I thought about the house, I heard Jesus say, "Get down on your knees and count the cost. This is not a game." Get down on my knees! Game? Who thought this was a game? Count the cost? What cost?

> "For which of you, intending to build a tower, does not sit down first and count the cost?"
>
> Luke 14:28, NKJV

This decision involved a giant leap of faith. As I prayed, I saw myself crawling to the edge of the Grand Canyon. I peered over, and the sight of the bottomless abyss made me dizzy. If I step off this ledge, I'll be obliterated with no chance of survival. It would be tantamount to suicide. There is no way I'll make it to the other side.

Yet, Jesus asked me to step out in faith with no safety net and walk on thin air. More than terrifying—this is insane!

"I don't know these people," I whined. "I don't know if I want to know these people. God, I don't know what I am doing." I lived a life of selfish indulgence. Yes, I wanted to know God, but I didn't believe I could do this.

If I gave my life to Jesus, I feared he would send me to some remote country with people I couldn't relate to. Instead, he found a mission field right here in Hollywood. As I thought about it, I realized Jesus had already started to work in my heart. Didn't I have several girls living with me? Didn't I want a bigger apartment? Hadn't my heart gone out to them?

I threw my hands up and said, "Fine, if you want to use this life, OK. It's yours. But you will have to do it through me because I have no idea what I am doing."

I heard God say with a grin, "Good. Because then I'll get all the glory."

I laughed and said, "You've got that right. You sure will."

What did I know about God? I had so much to learn. It would only be through him I could have any impact on these damaged lives. Despite the many confirmations I received, I looked for more. My flesh fought to hang on to its last remnants of control. I lay on my couch, wrestling with God, and hit upon an "aha" moment.

"OK, what about this? The School of Discipleship taught me you give us the peace that surpasses all understanding when you confirm what you're doing. Well, I have no peace, so this can't be you!"

I had a moment of smugness, thinking I had outsmarted God.

It's unclear how long I lay there. It might have been a minute or maybe an hour before I lifted my head and said, "Wait a minute? Wasn't there a near-hysterical girl here just a minute ago?" I had the peace that surpassed all understanding.

I couldn't even freak out about the fact I had the supernatural peace of God. When I laid my head back down, I slept better than I had in weeks.

If God had a purpose for my life, I wanted to find it. Isn't this what I prayed for when I received water baptism? Didn't I pray, "I will live the life you created me for? Today starts my new life with you." I guess this is it. This sure wasn't what I expected.

This became the final confirmation I needed to accept his leading into the most incredible adventure of my life. I had nothing left to wrestle against. I wanted to let Kleg know I would accept his offer to be the director of the woman's house.

Yes, I stepped off the edge. I looked up to Jesus, took a deep breath, and said, as Esther said in the Old Testament, "If I die, I die."

An astonishing thing happened as I stepped off that cliff into thin air. I stepped right into the palm of God's hand. While I couldn't see anything except my ultimate doom, God's hand became visible once I took a step of faith and carried me to the other side. *"Faith is the substance of things hoped for, the evidence of things not seen."* (Hebrews 11:1, NKJV).

Our true purpose—the only purpose worth pursuing—is to KNOW Jesus. The Hebrew Word for "know" is "yada". It carries a rich and multifaceted meaning going beyond simple intellectual understanding. "Yada" signifies a deep, intimate knowledge. It implies closeness and personal involvement, often used to describe the intimate relationship between a husband and wife. The pure, undefiled love that finds full acceptance in the beloved. It denotes an intimacy involving the whole being—mind, heart, and soul. All other questions align with pursuing that purpose: knowing God. My identity is defined, my confidence becomes unshakable, my compassion enlarges, and I have significance in my existence. Because I know who I am and have a sense of belonging, my heart is full of joy, for I am living in the safety of my Father's love. I thought I was pursuing Christ, but Christ was pursuing me.

If you find yourself at a crossroads, questioning your path and yearning for real answers, I invite you to take a step of faith. Challenge yourself to seek the truth earnestly. Open your heart to the possibility there is more to life than you see. Give God a chance to show you who He is. Take His Word literally, seek genuine connection, and be honest with your struggles. You might be surprised at how He responds to your quest for truth. Start today and let this journey be the beginning of a transformation that leads to a glorious adventure into the heart of God.

ABOUT THE AUTHOR

Pamela Rice is a licensed Marriage and Family Therapist with a Doctor of Ministry degree in applied Theology and has a private practice in Los Angeles, California. As a former program director for a clinical psychiatric unit, Pam understands human suffering and believes in the power of faith to transform lives and restore hope.

To learn more about my story, visit www.pamelaannrice.com or purchase my book, *Tarnished Crowns a Memoir: The Power of Purpose and Authenticity*, on Amazon.com.

CHAPTER FIVE

EL ROI- THE GOD WHO SEES ME

GINIA BISHOP

"**G**OD SAID IT'S TIME for you to heal," the minister said. I was shocked God used this beautiful woman to speak into my life and that He was attentive to the condition of my heart. I spent the past year at the altar of my church, searching for healing and freedom from the pain of my past. I prayed, worshipped, read books, cried, and begged God to move in my life. It appeared God kept silent every Sunday. One day, when I least expected it, God sent a minister to encourage and uplift me during prayer. She spoke about the pain I endured, pain I never told anyone about. At that moment, I felt hopeful God was answering my prayers. I wholeheartedly believed God was changing my life for the better.

Years went by before God began to unravel the layers of pain I carried deep within. It started with a presentation at Penn State York during Sexual Assault Awareness and Prevention Month.

"I felt dirty," the woman survivor explained. She told us she spent a long time in the shower to wash away the painful memories of abuse. As the woman told her story, my eyes grew wide in disbelief. "I felt that way too," I thought. After the presentation, I walked over to Kristen, the founder of Turning Point Counseling and Advocacy Center. I confided in her, something I've never shared with anyone; I felt the same way as the survivor who gave her testimony. Could it be that I, too, was a survivor of child sexual abuse? Kristen welcomed me with open arms and asked if I was ready to start my healing journey. Unbeknownst to me, healing would be the most difficult journey I would ever have to navigate. I did not know the adage, "Healing gets worse before it gets better."

During the following weeks, I decided to enroll in counseling. I did not know the depth of the pain I'd buried over the years. Once I began to revisit the painful memories, I could no longer deny or bury my childhood trauma. When I confronted my experiences of sexual abuse, I was invited to explore my relationship with my parents and the safety of my childhood home. I faced difficult truths and explored intense emotions. Honestly, I wasn't quite ready for this level of healing. It would be a few years down the road until I resumed counseling and invested the level of work (and tears) to find healing.

Broken Dreams

"I don't understand why you are comparing me to your past," my husband exclaimed. Truthfully, I did not fully understand the impact of my past trauma either. However, we both agreed I was not the woman I was before we married. Something changed. After marriage, I became withdrawn and shut down. My body tensed when my husband would try to touch me, even in a platonic way. I became combative when he tried to initiate sex. I felt shame when I used to experience joy and pleasure.

It was like someone flipped a switch in my life and hid it from me. We desperately tried to mend the broken pieces of my heart and mind. I could not awake from this nightmare. My husband watched helplessly as he lost the woman he'd come to know and love. During this time, I decided to give counseling another chance.

My counselor began to connect the dots between my broken marriage and my broken childhood. As a child, I longed for love and affection. While my parents were present, we were not close emotionally. According to Psychology Today, "Childhood emotional neglect happens when your parents fail to respond enough to your emotional needs as they raise you (emphasis mine)." Medical News Today adds, "Childhood neglect involves the absence of emotional responsiveness, nurturing, and engagement from caregivers." Over time, I learned children could become wounded when their parents are unavailable and disconnected. Or, when their parents show a lack of affection, encouragement, and emotional or psychological support.

There was a void in my heart God had created my parents to fulfill, but because of their brokenness and imperfections, the void remained and became deeper over time. I believed the lie that I was unloved because I felt insignificant to my parents: my father was not around consistently, and my mother was uninvolved due to her own trauma and struggle with addiction. When I turned twelve, I began looking for love in all the wrong places. I was taken advantage of by males overcome by lust, who never had my best interests at heart. At a young age, I associated love with sex. I believed I had nothing of value to offer other than a sexual relationship.

My husband was the first man who loved me beyond what I could offer him sexually. Yet, I struggled to receive his love and affection because it was foreign to my past experiences with the opposite sex. Adults who experienced childhood emotional neglect may have trust issues, difficulties embracing and maintaining new relationships, and challenges with communicating themselves effectively. Neither my husband nor I could imagine we would face intense emotional opposition so early in our marriage. We wondered if we had what it would take to make it another year.

THE WILDERNESS

When God spoke through the minister at church, I naively thought healing would happen instantaneously. I did not know the depths of my pain, nor I was prepared for the circumstances needed to bring about the healing I longed for. Like the Psalmist in the Bible, I began to walk through the valley of the shadow of death. Darkness surrounded me on all sides. On one hand, I had to come to terms with the reality of being a victim of sexual abuse. I battled the impact of sexual abuse on my marriage and mental health. On the other hand, I relived painful memories from my childhood interwoven with my present circumstances. The darkness of it all took a toll on me. During those years, I felt alone, depressed, and forgotten. I blamed myself for not being able to heal quickly, and hated what trauma stole from me and my family. I doubted God's ability to bring true and lasting freedom to my life.

Hagar is a woman in the Bible who knew what it felt like to be abandoned by those she loved and trusted. When we are introduced to Hagar, we are not told about the amazing woman she was. We do not learn of the desires and ambitions of her heart. We are immediately told Hagar was used by Sarai, Abram's wife, to conceive a child. Genesis 16:1, NKJV. I wish I could read Hagar's diary. I wondered how she felt at that moment. Was she elated to bear the child of Abram? Was she prepared to bear a child to present to Sarai to raise? Is this the idea of the family Hagar envisioned for herself as a young girl? I know there are significant cultural differences between the world Hagar lived in and the world you and I live in today, yet, as I read her story I wondered about the condition of Hagar's heart.

I continued to read Hagar's story, and I learned Hagar becomes pregnant and she gets into conflict with Sarai. She began to treat Sarai differently—with contempt. Sarai cries out to Abram, and Abram tells Sarai to deal with Hagar as she pleases. Sarai mistreated Hagar so badly that Hagar runs away to the desert. Have you ever found yourself alone in the wilderness? Were you the victim of someone else's poor decisions? Did you cry out to God in agony and despair, questioning how He could allow you to endure this much pain? I want you to know you are not alone in your experience. We were all affected by sin and brokenness, and we all have a story to tell.

What I love the most about Hagar's story is that God does not leave Hagar to fend for herself in the wilderness. Listen to this, "Now the Angel of the Lord found her by a spring of water in the wilderness..." (Genesis 16:7, NKJV) The Bible does not necessarily say Hagar sought the Lord in the wilderness. In fact, it says the complete opposite. The Angel of the Lord sought Hagar in what may have been the darkest season of her life. This spoke volumes to me about the love God has for His children. In a world filled with many people, God was attuned to the cries of Hagar's heart. Not only does the Angel of the Lord address Hagar's heart, but He also speaks life to her future. He tells Hagar she is with a child, and she is going to give birth to a son named Ishmael because the Lord has heard her affliction. I would like to note that while the Lord did not prevent Hagar's affliction, He was with her amid her afflictions. I love that Ishmael's name means "God hears." After this powerful encounter with the Lord, Hagar called the name of the Lord, "You-Are-the-God-Who-Sees." Or El Roi.

The God Who Sees Me

Like Hagar, life treated me harshly, and I found myself alone in the wilderness season. I cried, and I prayed to no end. I continued to attend counseling. There were times when I thought counseling only made everything worse. We were digging deep, exploring memories which only brought more pain. I reached out to friends. In my desperation, I even called crisis hotlines. Nothing I tried in this season of my life brought lasting relief. I had yet to come across the solution to my brokenness. I wanted to give up and run away from it all. In some ways, I did. I stopped putting forth the effort in counseling and healing. I thought to myself, "What is the point?" My marriage was not improving, and my mental and emotional health was at an all-time low. God felt so far away. Surely, the minister made a mistake. God was not healing me; He had rejected me just like everyone else.

One day, I came across a woman named Michelle who worked for a program named Bridges of Hope. I asked to schedule a meeting with her to learn more about her programs and their impact on women's lives in York County. I couldn't help but feel inspired as I listened to Michelle's vision for the program. We had a great time! We laughed and cried together as we reminisced about our journeys as wives and mothers. Before we ended the meeting, Michelle asked to pray with me, and I gave her my consent. In the middle of her prayer, she looks at me and says, "I feel led to ask for your forgiveness on behalf of your mother." She continues to pray and ask my forgiveness on behalf of my mother for many incidents that happened throughout the years, memories I had not thought of for a long time.

She prayed one of the most beautiful prayers I had ever received. More than the sincerity of her words, I felt the presence of God. This was the first time I met Michelle, and she did not know my story, let alone my most painful secrets. I knew she could only pray such a prayer if God Himself gave her the words to speak. In this moment, on a regular workday, God saw fit to speak to the condition of my heart.

While God did not address all of my problems and concerns during our meeting (we would've been there all night!), He spoke enough to reassure me I was not alone in the wilderness. In fact, He demonstrated through Michelle's prayer how He was present even when I was a child. The memories I had long ago buried and forgotten were still precious to God. He saw my tears, knew about the hidden pain, and intended to heal my heart just as He spoke to me years ago. God says in His Word that He is close to the brokenhearted. At that moment, I experienced the Bible coming to life. I left the meeting with renewed hope and faith for God to bring healing and freedom. I felt reassured of God's faithfulness, and I could trust Him to do as He promised in His perfect timing. This was a sacred moment for the little girl within me who felt rejected, used, and mistreated. I am reminded of the Scripture, "When my father and my mother forsake me, Then the LORD will take care of me." (Psalms 27:10, NKJV).

A Promise Kept

As I am writing to you today, approximately nine years after God invited me on the healing journey, I can testify God kept His promises to me. The Bible encourages us in Philippians 1:6 that He who began a good work in us will complete it! I am experiencing a level of restoration I never thought possible for someone like me. I am happily and healthily married. Through years of intense counseling, I found courage to release the shame of being sexually abused. I no longer feel dirty, but worthy of honor, love, and respect, and I released the false responsibility for the abuse. I know I am not to blame for what happened to me, and God does not blame me, either. (Romans 8:1, NKJV) I discovered my voice, learned how to communicate my wants and needs to others, and to be receptive to their acts of love and kindness. I am no longer plagued by the terrifying nightmares of being sexually abused or physically hurt. There are areas of my life that still require healing. For instance, I may become triggered by a certain touch, yet I am comforted knowing God is by my side through it all.

While God healed me from the pain of sexual abuse, He also led me down a path to forgiveness of my parents. I remember one day, while in prayer, God revealed to me held my parents hostage to a bad moment or a bad season in their lives. I remember thinking to myself, "What if my parents only viewed me as a teenage mother? Or what if they only viewed me through the lens of everything I've done wrong?" Through this example, God showed me my skewed perspective of my parents. With the help of His Holy Spirit, I began to release my parents from the unforgiveness I held in my heart. One of the most amazing miracles of my obedience is being able to share my story, Grace to Start Over, with my mother and receiving her apology for not being the mother I needed as a child. When I thought God abandoned me, He was working internally through my mom and me to bring about the changes we desired. Today, I can build a brand-new relationship with my mom. I can experience the love she is able to give.

Most of all, I am learning to love the woman I see in the mirror. Because I was emotionally neglected, I believed I did not matter. In turn, when I became an adult, I continued the cycle of neglecting myself. I sacrificed myself for the needs of others and poured into others without regard for my own well-being. I had poor boundaries and allowed others to walk all over me. With time, I understood the power of my voice. I realized I had the opportunity to teach others how I wanted to be treated. I could say, "No." Furthermore, I had the right to say no to people, places, and things hindering my healing process. I stopped seeing myself as a victim and started seeing myself as the daughter God loves. When I remembered my identity, I was reassured of the power and authority given to me by God when He created me in His image and likeness.

God is our Refuge

I pray my story infuses you with hope for a beautiful future. God tells us through the prophet Jeremiah, "For I know the thoughts that I think toward you, says the LORD, thoughts of peace and not of evil, to give you a future and a hope." (Jeremiah 29:11, NKJV) In what areas of your life do you feel abandoned or rejected by God? Have you become discouraged in the process of waiting for God's promises to come to pass in your life? Has it become difficult to believe God will bring you healing and freedom? I hope by now you know you are not alone. There are many of us who have endured the grueling season of inner healing and are able to testify God does indeed give "beauty for ashes".

Today, I want to invite you to surrender the ashes of your past to your loving Father God. Like me, you may be filled with anger, confusion, despair, and frustration. You may wonder how a loving God could allow you to experience so much pain. You may never want anything to do with God or His Church again. Can I let you in on a secret? God knows exactly how you feel, and He is not angry with you. His heart is filled with compassion. He knows you don't understand what is happening and you are seeking long-awaited answers. Yet, He knows how to work through this difficult season of your life to bring about good. (Romans 8:28, NKJV) I believe God wants to lift the heavy burdens you've carried for a long time. He wants you to taste His goodness, yes, even in the wilderness. He wants you to hear His songs of love and victory over you. Most importantly, He wants to remind you your story does not end here.

Activation

When hope's dream seems to drag on and on, the delay can be depressing. But when at last your dream comes true, life's sweetness will satisfy your soul. (Proverbs 13:12, TPT)

Where have you lost hope? What areas of your life need God's healing touch? Is there any pain or brokenness you would like to surrender to God in prayer? If so,

I encourage you to spend some time praying over and reflecting on the following journal prompts:

• What is one childhood memory still affecting me today?

• What is one thing causing me pain right now?

• What is one uncomfortable truth I need to face?

• What is one thing you would like God to know about the season of life you are in right now?

Dear God, I pray for the person who is reading this right now. I thank you for reminding them of your unconditional love. I thank you for providing them with the reassurance that you will never leave them nor forsake them. For your Word says you draw near to the brokenhearted. I thank you for being their ever-present help during their time of trouble. Thank you for being their refuge and safe space. Thank you, Father, for working behind the scenes to bring about the healing and freedom they so desperately long for. I pray, Lord, you will silence every lie of Satan. I declare Jeremiah 29:11 over this person today. They will not be destroyed, but they will see the future and the expected end You have for them, God. Touch their hearts and minds. I ask you to bring peace to the storms raging within them and to renew their perspective. I pray you will lead them to still waters. I thank you in advance, God, for the miracles and breakthroughs they will experience this year and for being a good and faithful Father. You tell us over again in your Word, God; we do not have to live in fear because you are with us. Lord, you told us if you are for us, who can be successful against us? Today, I pray you will refresh the weary soul. Let them place their hope in you again. In Jesus' name, I pray, Amen.

About the Author

Inspired by the redeeming power of God, I never thought my story could touch lives and bring hope and healing to others. As the Founder of Grace to Start Over Ministries, my passion is to support and empower hurting women to overcome the pain of their past. My journey led me to become a published author of "Grace to Start Over: You are worthy of a new beginning." Today, I am a proud speaker, Christian life coach, and mentor who believes every story can be rewritten and used to help others. I currently reside in Maryland with my husband and four lively and beautiful children. When I am not working, I love to get cozy with a good book, find new places to hang out with friends, and create lasting memories with my family.

Let's Connect

If you would like to join me on this path of healing and restoration, I invite you to follow me on social media @grace2startover. There, you will receive exciting updates on online courses, in-person events, life coaching opportunities, and book releases! If my story resonates with you, I encourage you to purchase Grace to Start Over: You are worthy of a new beginning. It is available online at Amazon and Barnes & Noble. If you want to share your story with me, I would love to interact via email at gracetostart@gmail.com.

Chapter Six

The Uncharted Uknown

Kerri-Ann Luketic

I didn't see this coming. A day when I would come into a place of mind-blowing discovery, causing my heart to come alive in knowing even though my eyes hadn't yet seen.

Perhaps this is what it's like for explorers. They know there is something to be found, and they know there is a gap between where they stand today and this other land in their heart. They feel it exists, but they haven't yet seen it with their own eyes or experienced its fullness, let alone articulated it for others to hear.

But as it is written:

> "Eye has not seen, nor ear heard, nor have entered into the heart of man. The things which God has prepared for those who love Him." But God has revealed them to us through His Spirit. For the Spirit searches all things, yes, the deep things of God.
>
> 1 Corinthians 2:9-10, NKJV

I have had this expanding love for words rising from within me over the years. The more time I spend with Yahweh the more I find I'm wanting to discover points of origin, especially in words. The word 'uncharted' is one of my favourites. To be uncharted is all about the unknown and, by definition, is not shown or located on a map[1]; unexplored as a place or region. The word refers to anything that isn't plotted or planned and expresses a wider unknown. Equally in the physical and nonphysical senses, it can mean "not yet mapped, surveyed, or investigated."[2]

I feel the word uncharted encapsulates the scripture in 1 Corinthians above, in that we have an invitation to go off the map to explore the things God has prepared for us, and Holy Spirit is keen to be our guide. These unknown spaces our eyes haven't yet seen, and our ears haven't yet heard, but there is this magnetic pull drawing us into the awe and wonder of the unseen, unknown.

Now, like many others, I have to say I have frequently questioned in my thoughts whether I was truly hearing God speak. There would always be a doubt in my mind as I weighed and checked and weighed again what I thought I was hearing, seeing, knowing, or sensing. I have known what it's like to be stuck in a 'round the mountain' thought space of doubt, having gathered plenty of evidence to suggest I needed to question my interpretive abilities. I felt I couldn't rely on my intuition or my knowing for what I was perceiving.

My thoughts would collide in a mix of …

"Is that God? Or is this me?"

"Where did that thought come from?"

"What am I meant to do with this thought?"

"What if I get it wrong, people are going to think I'm crazy!"

"Is this really you, Lord?"

Traversing this well-worn pathway had only ever led me to the same places of clenched teeth, anxiety, and energy drain. It shifted, however when I decided to step over the invisible line in my mind landscape and leave the mountain of doubt, crossing into the land of belief. I discovered there were so many places of thought exploration waiting for me. A whole new world of experiences, conversations, questions, and discovery awaited!

Why am I saying all this? Because I want to invite you into an uncharted, explorative, wonder-filled space of experience with the Lord, where we embrace and fully believe everyone can hear Yahweh's voice, and everyone can see what He sees.

Consider these two scriptures for a moment:

> *"My sheep hear My voice, and I know them, and they follow Me."*
> John 10:27, NKJV

> *"Then Jesus answered and said to them, "Most assuredly, I say to you, the Son can do nothing of Himself, but what He sees the Father do; for whatever He does, the Son also does in like manner."*
> John 5:19, NKJV

As the ones who are created in His image and have Jesus as our living example, whatever He does, we get to do, and we get to do things that are even greater still. I want to invite you to embrace these truths and allow your heart and mind to rest in them. Breathe them in. Allow them to bring peace to your body and stillness to your mind as I share with you a moment of encounter:

I remember a day, where I was being intentional to have communion with the Lord. It was midday, and I sank into my lounge with tears in my eyes, fully aware of Him being so present with me in that moment. The song "Communion"[3] by Maverick City Music played in the background as I paused my day to commune with Him—to be present and to be in love with Him. Jesus gently and lovingly sat down beside me, and I leant in close to rest my head upon His shoulder. That moment of love and comfort is always 'beyond words' beautiful. This is where I LOVE to be.

I rest and I know, He is my King.

In this place of rest, I see in my mind a broom, sweeping the floor, sweeping up all the dust. And I know it's Jesus holding the broom. I ask Him, "Would you make my dust into a star?" He lovingly responds, "No, I'll make a nebula."

This might seem like a strange conversation to have, but it made so much sense to me. We had been talking about stars and space, about the birthing of stars, and I knew stars were created with space dust and gases.

Now before I go further into this moment, I want to rewind my story a little. In the early days of my faith journey, I thought I was broken. I felt that my 'see in the spirit' screen wasn't working, and my direct line to hearing the voice of the Lord was out of order. It was like the silent black abyss was my portion for the most part, therefore, I wasn't going to have those kinds of mind-blowing spiritual experiences I had heard of. It made sense to just give up trying, as it seemed to be impossible. Fortunately, my curiosity and desire were far greater, and I just knew, like an explorer knows, there has to be more to experience.

I deeply yearned for 'encounters' with Yahweh. I wanted to see Him, experience Him, to be in His presence so badly that I kept searching for Him in the stories of others who had had the experiences I wanted to have. I read books, went to meetings, watched movies, anything to try bringing illumination to my eyes and a frequency to my ears, allowing me to experience the spiritual realities of the unseen realm of God and His kingdom.

In my search, I feel so deeply in love with the Lord. Our relationship bloomed, and I could feel myself being taught by Him. Something I've found to be so incredible, divine, and mind-blowing. I mean, here was the God of the universe teaching me new things about himself, about myself, and about His kingdom I never knew. This might be a strange thing to say, because of course the Lord would want to teach us new things, but truly, I always thought it was the pastor who taught or the elder who carried the wisdom, not little me through the inspired teachings of Holy Spirit.

> *"But the Helper, the Holy Spirit, whom the Father will send in My name, He will teach you all things, and bring to your remembrance all things that I said to you."*
>
> John 14:26, NKJV

When I began to recognise the many ways Holy Spirit would interact with me to teach me, it was like a million little light bulbs went off connecting dots and highlighting revelation that had always been there, waiting for my discovery. I particularly remember one profound learning experience. It was with a dear friend in a coffee shop. She was the kind of friend who I considered a spiritual mum. One who I could talk to about what I was experiencing with God, as best as I could articulate, and she would listen without judgment, offer encouragement, insight, and wisdom. This moment was a very illuminating experience, and I find it helpful to break it down into three parts when sharing.

As my friend and I sat chatting together in this beautiful coffee shop enjoying our favourite drinks, she asked me a very simple question.

"Do you have a word for me?"

She knew I was learning and developing my spiritual intelligence and understanding, but in this moment, I have to say her question caught me off guard. To clarify, she was asking for a word, as in an insightful, prophetic, knowledgeable word received from the Lord to share with her to bring confirmation and/or encouragement. I stopped for a minute to 'look and see' what the Lord might want to show or say to me for my friend. I engaged my imagination and revelation space, and what I saw was a muted dark grey colour. There wasn't much shape or form within the colour at first. It felt like if there was any detailed imagery, it was way back there—far away from me and right out of focus.

I've come to learn when we are practising with Holy Spirit, He can often give us a partial image or word, then He waits to see what we will do with it. From a simple colour to even a deep feeling associated with a fuzzy image. I'm more than happy to learn through a space of growing trust, but in this moment with my friend, it genuinely felt as if there was nothing there to share. Perhaps I could even word it like this. I couldn't quite pull in what I was experiencing to a place of articulation that would make sense to my friend (again like the explorer in the beginning of this chapter). And so, my pause lasted a decent amount of time as I considered all this and then I responded.

"No, No word."

I had no more clarity in the greyness, so I believed there was nothing there, which surely meant I didn't have a word or picture, a knowing, or a sense for my friend. But Holy Spirit was committed to making this a teachable moment for me. As my friend questioned again, "Are you sure?" The initial greyness began to lighten a little. There were a few lines coming into the picture, faint outlines of something there, but mostly still very grey.

In these moments, time is really seconds, and yet in those seconds, so much is happening it can feel like days moving behind the scenes. My cool, calm but somewhat puzzled exterior was no indication of the number of questions, enquiries, investigations, and wonderings taking place internally. My spiritual ears were listening acutely, and my spiritual eyes were looking deeply into what was being presented. And yet, no words came to describe what was happening.

Sensing that I wasn't getting anywhere fast, my friend then said,

"Oh, it's just that I'm moving my business..."

And then, as if suddenly, the seemingly all-grey image became detailed enough for me to realise what I was seeing, and the revelation light bulb came on! I was seeing her old office window with her business name and her business contact details printed in big bold print as if I were standing outside her office looking in. Only in my image, her signage was all blacked out. It wasn't clear. Instead, it was covered over in black like a Sharpie pen had been used to block it all out, and my spirit could testify to the confirmation of her moving. I could see the image now, CLEARLY, with focus.

It was at this point I knew I needed to allow the image to develop. It wasn't that I had nothing to share, rather like a camera's negative film developing, the images, visions, feelings, and knowing the Lord wanted to bring me into needed some time and freedom to come into focus.

There is power in the pause.

In the pause, the imagery and knowings begin to develop. When we practice with safe friends, we can move inside our imagination with the Lord to bring about the revealing—asking questions, allowing depth to be perceived, and trusting our inspired intuition. This is incredible because it gives a foundational framework for encounters to multiply in our care and stewardship.

When I think about this profound lesson with Holy Spirit, I wonder how many times I have seen, known, heard, or perceived something in the spirit but disregarded it because it didn't make any sense. It was an unknown, or it just seemed like nothing was happening. In essence, I hit the manual override button and shut down the experience because it made no sense, lacked understanding, wasn't clear, or just didn't seem to hold any substance.

When I've worked with clients in the exploration of seeing in the Spirit, we occupy the space of seeing by allowing ALL our senses to be engaged, because seeing isn't restricted to just our spiritual eyes, it's a multi-sensory experience. I think this is where many have gotten stuck thinking encounters don't happen for them. We all experience heavenly realities in varied ways, so we truly must allow our senses to be trained and our conscious awareness to expand to facilitate the flow of revelation through our unique, tailor-made spiritual receptors (our body, soul, and spirit).

> *"But solid food is for the mature, whose spiritual senses perceive heavenly matters. And they have been adequately trained by what they've experienced to emerge with understanding of the difference between what is truly excellent and what is evil and harmful."*
>
> Hebrews 5:14, TPT

In this conversation, the most common place of uncertainty we land in is the realm of the unknown, uncharted, and indescribable. So often we find this space emerging within that goes beyond words and far beyond our understanding. This is why we can say things like, "I know the Lord is revealing something to me, I just don't have the words for it yet." Or maybe we can sense revelation coming and have an awareness of it being in and around us, with glimpses of a theme like it has something to do with rest, but when we try to pull it all together coherently, we just can't fully grasp it. It's like, "It's on the tip of my tongue."

In my coaching sessions with clients, we always pause to give our understanding to the Lord, so it doesn't cause us to shut down, disengage, and close off to what the Lord wants to reveal. We intentionally choose to engage in peace in this moment.

> *"And the peace of God, which surpasses all understanding, will guard your hearts and minds through Christ Jesus."*
>
> Philippians 4:7, NKJV

> *"Then God's wonderful peace that transcends human understanding, will guard your heart and mind through Jesus Christ."*
>
> Philippians 4:7, TPT

Allowing peace to guard our hearts and minds is a beautiful practise of trust in Holy Spirit. It gives grace for our hearts to open to the things of the spirit our minds don't yet fully comprehend and therefore gives us some breathing room within an encounter experience. Revelation now has an opportunity to come forth uninhibited, bypassing our conscious and subconscious minds for a moment to find a landing strip in our hearts. This is so important as we train our minds to serve us well and allow our spirits to lead us into new, exciting spaces and places of encounter.

The next thing that has the potential to happen is when doubt shows up to talk us out of what we are experiencing. We may begin to question what's happening through the lens of "This is so weird," or "You might think this is crazy if I told you," or "This can't be right!" Questions causing you to disregard, turn away from, or categorise the experience as not being from the Lord are limiting. Rather, questions that welcome curiosity and wonder are powerful, as they will take us into a deeper, wider, more expansive space inside our experience with the Lord.

Some brilliant questions to ask as you move through an encounter moment with the Lord are:

Yahweh, what do you want to show me? Tell me more, Lord.

- What do you want to highlight today?

- Where is 'wonder' in this moment?

- In this encounter, where do I feel most alive?

- What do I 'know' in this moment? Stop and consider what your knower, knows.

- Who is with you in this encounter? Look around in your imagination and sense, know, or see who is joining you. It is possible to find there are two or three gathered with you, more than you originally see or know. It's powerful to 'look around' and increase your scope of view.

- What do you now see or know you didn't see or know at the beginning of the encounter? Has something new emerged? Revelation grows and expands, and an encounter will too. Taking a moment to allow for new revelation to come is important.

- There are also some important things to notice happening during an encounter.

- Do you feel any sensations in your body? Like warmth on your hands or bubbles on your forehead.

- What were you seeing/knowing when those sensations were happening?

- What emotions are you feeling in this moment?

- Which of your senses are engaging with this encounter and in what way?

I hope you find these questions and thoughts helpful for moving into a deeper, more connected experience with the Lord.

Now back to my original encounter in communion with Jesus—the dust and the broom. I could easily have laughed and thought it was weird because it seemed so random. Yet, I have a history of holding these spaces with Him, and even more so in this particular conversation.

I chose to go deeper. Some may say I went off on a tangent, or down a rabbit trail, thinking there's nothing in it. But for me, eternity is in this encounter. I took the time to explore and gain understanding. Remember how Jesus said he was making a nebula? A nebula is a giant cloud of dust and gas in space. Some nebulae (more than one nebula) come from the gas and dust thrown out by the explosion of a dying star, such as a supernova. Other nebulae are regions where new stars are beginning to form. For this reason, some nebulae are called "star nurseries."[4]

This for me is weighty revelation.

It caused me to remember a conversation with another beautiful friend of mine who said the words "mind blown" had her think of a star exploding—the greatness and expansion. To think stars form from dust in space and then to see the Lord not want to just take my dust and throw it in the bin or even make a star but instead to begin to create a space for a star nursery just speaks so much encouragement to my heart for the increase in revelation opening up like millions of light bulb moments but also the birthing of revelation coming from our hearts desire to experience more of Him.

Here's the thing, these encounters are never meant to be one-offs, they are designed as an invitation to revisit, see again, explore things that may have been out of focus the first time you had the encounter, to gain greater understanding and depth in knowing, to listen for new sounds, to feel different emotions, and to hold an increased capacity in its expression in and through you.

Remember how Paul prayed for the spirit of wisdom and revelation in Ephesians 1:

> "And [I pray] that the eyes of your heart [the very centre and core of your being] may be enlightened [flooded with light by the Holy Spirit] so that you will know and cherish the hope [the divine guarantee, the confident expectation] to which He has called you, the riches of His glorious inheritance in the saints (God's people),"
>
> Ephesians 1:18, AMP

The Passion Translation articulates it this way:

> "I pray that the light of God will illuminate the eyes of your imagination, flooding you with light, until you experience the full revelation of the hope of his calling—that is, the wealth of God's glorious inheritances that he finds in us, his holy ones!"
>
> Ephesians 1:18, TPT

The eyes of our hearts or the eyes of our imagination need light. They experience, know, and have the capacity to receive illuminating light. Opening our hearts to receive revelatory light is a process of giving our minds permission to rest, not figure everything out, not over analyse what the Lord is imparting to us that has come from a realm beyond what we experience here on earth. It allows us the opportunity to come into a space of 'revelating' with Him as we engage the unseen realms of Heaven.

Ka-Pow! Mind-Blown!!

I truly didn't see this kind of revelation coming, but my heart comes alive inside this conversation, and I know there is so much more to see and experience here. A lot of our experiences are going to exponentially increase as we explore, share, articulate, and expand together.

Today, as you read this, take a moment now to breathe deeply. Take a pause moment and enjoy being still in His presence. Be still and know Him. Breathe deep again and speak peace and comfort over your mind, your body, and your soul.

"Peace be still, mind. Yahweh is here."

"Peace be still body, it's ok. Yahweh is surely here."

"Peace be still."

This is what I pray as I pause, acknowledging Father's presence as I turn my heart's affections toward Him, and then I'm giving my mind permission to be at peace and releasing my spirit to take the lead, instead of my understanding.

And then ask Him, "Lord, what would you like to show me today?"

Wait, look, and see. I'm sure you'll be surprised by what is illuminated in the eyes of your imagination as you experience the uncharted unknown of His kingdom.

NOTES

1. Merriam-Webster Dictionary

2. Dictionary.com

3. Communion, by Maverick City Music, featuring Steffany Gretzinger and Brandon Lake

4. https://spaceplace.nasa.gov/nebula/en/

About the Author

Kerri-Ann Luketic is a passionate storyteller, a Transformational Life Coach, and dynamic speaker with over 20 years' experience in transformational success principles. As a certified coach with the Brave Thinking Institute, she specializes in helping intuitively inspired women build their dreams, accelerate their results, and magnify their message to create lives they love.

In her latest book, "Hearing God in the Noise", Kerri-Ann shares her personal journey of overcoming spiritual noise to live in the truth of her identity in Jesus. Her personal stories and spiritual insights reveal the Lord's love and His desire for each of His beloved to hear, see, and know Him.

Kerri-Ann's coaching programs and workshops are designed to help you break through limiting thought paradigms to reveal the pathway to living a life you love. Whether through her inspiring book or transformative coaching, Kerri-Ann will empower you to create a life filled with love, joy, adventure, and overflowing abundance.

You can connect with Kerri-Ann here: www.kaluketic.com

And on Socials here:
Facebook: @k.a.luketiclifecoach
Instagram: @k.a.luketic
YouTube: @K.A.Luketic

Resources:

Get instant access to Chapter 3 of Kerri-Ann's book, Hearing God in the Noise, for Free here:
www.hearinggod.kaluketic.com/freechapter

Get your very own copy of Hearing God in the Noise here:
https://www.amazon.com.au/dp/1738571602

Chapter Seven

How Jesus Set Me Free from Guilt and Condemnation

Paula Burr

Life Before My Encounter with God

It wasn't like I didn't believe in God. He was always there for me from quite early on in my life. I would pray to Him when I was in trouble, and I had the feeling he knew what I was thinking and feeling and somehow understood me. When I was at school and Sunday School, I heard about Jesus and others in the bible. There were stories about missionaries—women who went by themselves to different countries to tell others about Jesus and show His love to them. These people inspired me, and I wanted to be like them.

There came a time after my confirmation in the church when I lived a life involving keeping the rules, attending church, trying to live by the sermon on the mount, and trying to improve myself. I thought this was being a Christian, and I wanted to do everything right. At first, I got satisfaction from it, but after a while,

I became a very mechanical sort of person and didn't really feel anything anymore. After a time, I began to wonder if I was right with God.

Somehow, I had the feeling He was not pleased with me because I couldn't keep all His rules. This was especially true of those set forth in the Sermon on the Mount, where we are told to keep them in our hearts as well as outwardly. I felt trapped because I knew enough about God to understand what He wanted, but I was in despair because I couldn't do it. There is no way to escape God, even in death. I knew God was who my heart sought, as my heart wasn't satisfied with anything less.

In Ecclesiastes, a book in the Old Testament, it says God has put eternity in our hearts, that's why anything less will not satisfy. But how could I enjoy His presence if I felt condemned because I couldn't do what I knew was right in my heart? When I committed my life to Christ at my confirmation, I meant it with all my heart. I renounced all the evil in my life and promised to serve Jesus for the rest of my life. This was going to be 'it'—the life I'd always wanted. I was very happy enjoying being part of the church I attended and celebrating communion regularly with my friends. I even participated in post-confirmation classes because I found the Bible studies we did so fascinating.

In my enthusiasm, I set out on a big project for self-improvement. I worked hard at school and managed to up my exam results considerably enough to get a progress prize. Due to more consistent practice, my violin playing improved enough to pass a music examination. I became much more self-disciplined, and I also went on a diet when I found out I weighed a lot more than I thought. This was encouraged by my family to begin with, but when I lost too much, they became concerned as I became thinner. In addition, I sank into a deep depression because my life began to lose any meaning. It was just like the times as a child when I had been playing contentedly in the sunshine when a dark cloud would suddenly creep over the sun, making it grow dark and cold. I found no meaning in any of my achievements and lost enthusiasm for family get-togethers, increasingly withdrawing from other people. Feeling frozen inside, existing through my daily routine. I looked forward to bedtime, when I could go to sleep and escape from everything. Having enthusiastically tried to make my life perfect, I found

I couldn't do it. No matter how closely I followed Jesus, there was no assurance I was right with Him and would wander around locally under a heavy sense of condemnation. I tried to escape Him but found I couldn't. It seemed God was hunting me down, and there was nowhere to go. The joy I had experienced when I turned to Him at my confirmation turned into endless torment.

How is My Life Now?

So, my early to middle teens had been ones of descending into despair, but an encounter with God one evening was the beginning of a new journey for me. Since then, He has shown me how His love is not based on my performance or adherence to rules, but on His grace and mercy. God's acceptance of me has given me hope, meaning, and purpose. My identity is not the sum of everything I had been labelled with. I am His child, and I know God loves me not just because I believe it in my head, but because I know His love inwardly in my heart. Instead of the depression and despair I had been feeling, I now have a deep assurance for the present and the future. God is the most real thing about my life. He is not a hound who I dread, but a loving shepherd who leads me through life and provides all I need to live out the destiny He originally planned for me. Over the years, I have learned to listen to His voice, speaking in my spirit or through words from the Bible. He tells me He loves me and points out things need to change. Sometimes, I feel prompted to ring or speak to someone, visit someone, or share something encouraging with someone else. Sometimes, He wants to show me how much He loves me. My life is different because my decisions and actions stem from the relationship I have with Him. I notice the difference when I try to act independently of God. It doesn't usually work! The other great thing I've experienced since then is even though I'm going through a bad experience, God is there for me and can comfort me in a way no one else can if I turn to Him for support. Sometimes, I think I know better and have tried my way in a situation, but it usually brings more trouble or sorrow, and I end up going to Him for help. He has always drawn especially close to me at significant moments in my life, and this comfort has strengthened me to endure the situation. When another voice tells me lies about God or me, I know not to listen but to heed the voice of Jesus. He tells us His sheep hear His voice, He knows them, and they follow Him.

Even when life has been difficult and I've felt down, Jesus has shown me how to overcome these situations.

> *Blessed be the LORD, my rock, who trains my hands for war, and my fingers for battle;*
>
> Psalm 144:1, ESV

Even when I've blown it, God has not cast me off but is just waiting for me to come back and be close to Him again. He has told me He will complete what He's started in me, and I have the glorious hope of an eternal relationship with Him and eventually becoming like Him when I meet Him face to face.

When God speaks to me, it is not in a booming voice or a blinding light. It is in the quiet moments of my life when I feel His presence and hear His gentle whispers guiding me.

My Life-Changing Experience with Jesus Christ

In the earlier part of my life, I thought I knew all there was to know about Jesus, and what I knew of Him was as good as it got. I used to wish I had an experience as life-changing as the missionaries I had read about, Gladys Alward and Isabel Kuhn. Their stories inspired me and made me want to do something adventurous like they did, but I thought maybe it was for a special few.

As I described earlier, when I was confirmed, I really meant it when I said in the vows, "I turn to Christ." I eagerly embraced the lifestyle of going to church, taking communion, praying at night, and getting involved in the community, including teaching Sunday School.

HOW JESUS SET ME FREE FROM GUILT AND CONDEMNATION

One evening, I went to a meeting of those involved in Sunday School at the house of the superintendent, and it took the form of a bible study on John Chapter 1. We looked at the passage where John the Baptist was pointing to Jesus:

> *"Behold, the Lamb of God, who takes away the sin of the world."*
>
> John 1:29, ESV

Now, I had heard this verse many times at the communion services I regularly attended, but somehow, on this occasion, the words took on a life of their own. I sensed in my spirit that Jesus was talking to me, saying, 'I know you can't do it. That's why I died for you.' This was the first time I experienced God speaking to me directly through the bible. He felt more real than I'd ever experienced before. I had read the verse because it was something I was supposed to do as a Christian. It was quoted weekly at the communion service but I had never experienced it as a living word stirring my heart. The truth percolated through as I realised I hadn't really applied what He'd done for me. I had believed it in my head, but that was as far as it went. These words now pierced my heart and gave the assurance I was forgiven and not under condemnation. I needed to trust in what Jesus did for me on the cross to enjoy a relationship with God with no barriers. That evening, there was also a discussion about Jesus baptising in the Spirit, which I didn't fully grasp at the time, but it created in me a longing to be filled with more and more of God in my life.

I felt a ray of hope beaming into the darkness and the load I had been carrying around felt like it had lifted. In addition, I felt a deep hunger for more, especially to read the bible more now that some verses seemed to pop out and lodge themselves in my spirit. This was a spiritual awakening to a life that was there, but that I was only beginning to experience for myself. The sense of meaninglessness was gone as I became aware of being part of a bigger story beyond my earthly life. I was no longer trying to carry my burden alone.

In a second-hand bookshop, I found a small book with a poem in it called The Hound of Heaven, by Francis Thompson. This poem echoed the feeling I had as

I was seeking God, but also fleeing Him because I felt fear and condemnation. At the end of the poem, the writer describes how God found him:

All which I took from thee I did but take,
Not for thy harms,
But just that thou mightst seek it in My arms.

All which thy child's mistake
Fancies as lost, I have stored for thee at home:
Rise, clasp My hand, and come!'
Halts by me that footfall:
Is my gloom, after all,
Shade of His hand, outstretched caressingly?

Rather than hunting me down, now, He was drawing me with his cords of love. There was no condemnation but a sense of His loving presence, which would not let me go.

Following that Bible Study, I started attending a similar group on Saturday evenings, which became a lifeline for me. The gentle love shown by the group, the worship, and the reading of the Bible, which had come to life for me after that wonderful evening, became a lifeline for me, though God still had much work and healing to do in my life.

A few months later, I attended a service where a group called 'The Fisher Folk' was leading the worship. They asked us to use any noisy things we had on us, such as keys, to join in with the accompaniment. There was a talk I can't remember much about, but I did go up at the end of the message for the laying on of hands, so I could be filled with the Spirit. I sensed another great reassurance as the person ministering said God's hand was on my life. I had been listening too much to the devil, and they gave me a verse, which I later found out was from the book of Isaiah.

> *And your ears shall hear a word behind you, saying, "This is the way, walk in it."*
>
> Isaiah 30:21, ESV

God had shown me just what I needed to know. When He wanted to take me further, He would tell me what I needed to know at each stage. In the days following, when I was doing ordinary things like working at school or being with friends and family, I felt a deep joy in my heart. It was so wonderful having experienced God's touch in my life.

What My Experience Taught Me

My experience taught me that God is very different from how I imagined Him. He was not some tyrant wanting to catch me out. I did not appreciate how much He loved me or the tenacity of His love. God didn't give up on me because I couldn't get it right. He kept pursuing me until I had to surrender when He showed me how it was for me that He died, and I was never going to be up to standard on my own. Approval by God didn't depend on me being a good girl, but just on His love for me, which opened a way to be close to Him without dread or condemnation.

After experiencing God at the service I went to, I sought to listen to what He was telling me rather than the enemy's accusing words or other sources. I would like to have always listened to Him, but I found it was too easy to be misled or do what I wanted to do because I didn't trust that God knew best. Reading God's truth in the Bible, being quiet before God in listening mode, and allowing the Holy Spirit to guide me helped me better discern the sources of guidance. I found that God always encouraged me, even if He needed to put a few things right. If the voice was accusing and condemnatory, it came from the enemy. I learned it was important to sift and test what people told me was from God against the truth, so I wouldn't be led away from my precious relationship with God and end up back to keeping rules.

GOD IN MY EVERYDAY LIFE

God becoming real in my life was a gift from Him, but I've found that I've needed to nurture the relationship. If I rush about my life, forgetting about God most of the time, the sense of His presence in my life can start to fade. It's so easy to forget, so I need to be intentional about making time spent with God a priority, just as you need to spend time with a spouse, child, or friend to maintain a relationship with them.

The beginning of the day is an especially important time of day because how we start the day affects how the day goes. Setting time apart to be with God to listen to Him by reading the bible and committing my day to Him helps me to include Him in all I do during the day. It ensures I get God's perspective on all that's going to happen during the day. I also find that some praise and thanksgiving are good, positive starts to the day. There have been times when I've had to be quite creative due to circumstances such as looking after babies and small children or going to work early and travelling. Consciously turning to God during the day helps to grow closer to Him. Intimacy with God through fellowship with Him in prayer at special times of the day and during the busyness of the day is key to maintaining a beautiful friendship with Him and living a fruitful life.

I also find that even a short time of consciously turning to God through prayer, music, or a short devotional is a good way to end the day before going to sleep. Sometimes, I look back on things I was grateful for and review how I reacted to events to ensure I don't go to sleep with any unfinished business with Him.

One of my favourite verses, which has stayed with me throughout my journey with the Lord, is:

One thing have I desired of the LORD, that will I seek: That I may dwell in the house of the LORD all the days of my life, to behold the beauty of the LORD, and to enquire in his temple. (Psalm 27:4, NKJV)

Spending time with God is not something I do because I must, but because it is a delight when He is real to me. This is so different from before He became so real to me. Somehow, it seems natural to spend time praising and worshipping Him.

When I've felt myself drifting back into focusing more on daily routines, I talk to God about it and ask Him to renew my passion for Him.

As I've got to know Him better, hope has grown in me as I see how He brings me through challenging circumstances.

How Is It with You?

What is your experience with God? Perhaps you've been part of a church for years, but it's just become routine. Maybe you're heavily involved in your church, but there is no joy in what you're doing. Do you have an assurance of God's forgiveness and a sure hope of an eternal relationship with Him? What does God mean to you?

If you are struggling as I was, know that God has provided a way forward for you. God sees your struggles and your desire to please Him. He knows we will never make it on our own trying to please Him because we have a natural tendency to think we can, but not the power to do it. He sees the misery we are in because we've chosen independence from Him. I tried my hardest and still felt condemned until God graciously opened the eyes of my heart. Ultimately, God is good and sees our hearts. He knows all about us, our thoughts, and our longings. When He sees how passionately we are seeking Him, He will be found because He is the one who puts the desire to seek Him in our hearts.

> *And you will seek me and find me when you search for me with all your heart.*
>
> Jeremiah 29:13, NKJV

God does not expect us to make it on our own. The Jews, with all their laws and ceremonies, could not earn favour with God. The Apostle Paul considered himself a former Pharisee of Pharisees, so we aren't going to improve on that. Instead, we look to Jesus, the Lamb who takes away the sin of the world through

His selfless love demonstrated by an excruciating death on the cross, which says, "I did this for you because I know you can't do it by yourself."

How Do I Apply This to Myself?

A passage in the bible I found threw light on what I was experiencing in the book of Romans, chapters 7 and 8. Read through these slowly, allowing the words to sink in. Ask the Holy Spirit to open the eyes of your heart and allow yourself to experience the breakthrough taking place in these verses. When I read these verses, I found the passage resonated with what was going on inside of me. By this, I mean suffering the conflict of wanting to do the right thing but finding myself unable to do it, but then the light is turned on as Romans 7 leads into Romans 8. There is no condemnation because Jesus has set me free from the law of sin and death

> *For I delight in the law of God, in my inner being, but I see in my members another law waging war against the law of my mind and making me captive to the law of sin that dwells in my members. Wretched man that I am! Who will deliver me from this body of death? Thanks be to God through Jesus Christ our Lord! So then, I myself serve the law of God with my mind, but with my flesh I serve the law of sin.*
>
> Romans 7:22-25, ESV

> *There is, therefore, now no condemnation for those who are in Christ Jesus. For the law of the Spirit of life has set you free in Christ Jesus from the law of sin and death.*
>
> Romans 8:1-2, ESV

The first verse of Romans 8 became my favourite verse, and I would quote it often to remind myself when I felt condemned. In fact, the whole of Romans 8 is wonderful because it describes so fully what God has done for us in removing condemnation from us and giving us a new life led by the Spirit. God's Spirit confirms our new identity as He enables us to cry 'Abba Father.'

Spend time reading and marinating in Romans 8; there is so much to lift and encourage us. Declare it out loud when you feel overwhelmed with guilt and condemnation, speaking the truth to your soul and not listening to condemning lies, saying you'll never be good enough for God. Put notes with these verses in places where you will see them regularly. At the end of Romans 8, there is a wonderful description of how there is nothing in all creation that can separate us from the love of God in Christ Jesus.

I've also found that it is helpful to connect with others with whom you can share and who can encourage you.

And let us consider how we may spur one another on toward love and good deeds.
Hebrews 10:24, NIV

It's so important to be surrounded by fellow Christians who we can trust to help us to become who God created us to be without condemnation.

Going Deeper

If you want to continue to enjoy the freedom of living a life led by the Spirit, an excellent strategy is to meditate regularly on the truth about our identity in God. This involves daily reading the Bible and making a note of any words that particularly speak to you. Write them down and journal about them and find creative ways to build them into your life, perhaps through bible journalling, memorisation, or writing poems or songs about them or listening to songs about them. This wonderful store of truth you are imbibing each day will strengthen you against any lies thrown at you and give you hope when you are struggling. The passage below is one I've found particularly helpful on which to meditate. It allows the truth to sink in that it is not my performance of keeping the rules but trusting in Jesus that counts and all He's accomplished for us, so we become new people led by His Spirit.

In Matthew's gospel, Jesus invites those who feel burdened by religion to come to Him and take His yoke upon them instead of the heavy one they are carrying. As soon as you start to feel burdened by rule-keeping and religious rituals, just come to Jesus and take His yoke. Picture Him taking your heavy yoke and placing His on you. Be led by Him and find that He is not a hard taskmaster but a loving, compassionate shepherd.

> *"Are you tired? Worn out? Burned out on religion? Come to me. Get away with me, and you'll recover your life. I'll show you how to take a real rest. Walk with me and work with me—watch how I do it. Learn the unforced rhythms of grace. I won't lay anything heavy or ill-fitting on you. Keep company with me, and you'll learn to live freely and lightly."*
>
> Matthew 11:28-30, MSG

Meditate on these words, letting them sink in. I pray for you to experience the fullness of God's love in your life and know the rest that comes from giving all your burdens to Him and living a life in the Spirit free of condemnation. God is on your side, and nothing can separate us from His love.

ABOUT THE AUTHOR

My name is **Paula Burr**, and I am a follower of Jesus, a grandmother, an enthusiastic reader and writer, and a passionate amateur violinist. I enjoy spending time with my family and making music at church and in the community. Currently, I live in a small town in Sussex on the South Coast of England with a lively cocker spaniel and a laid-back cat. The area is not far from the sea and boasts some fantastic woodland and downland walks.

When God touched my life many years ago, it made a profound difference in me. Since then, He has been with me through many life events which could have overwhelmed me, but He brought me through them all. I am motivated to share what He has done for me to encourage others and bring hope into their lives. Life can be bewildering and knock us off course, so I want to share the tools and insights God has given me to help others face the challenges of life with hope.

My passion is empowering individuals to unlock their full potential, and I am dedicated to supporting Christians on their journey to overcome challenges and grow in their walk with Jesus. I would love to hear from you. If you have questions or want to share your experiences, feel free to contact me at paulaann71@paulaburr.uk or visit my blog at paulaburr.uk.

Chapter Eight

Breaking into Brokenness- Bringing Beauty Out of Ashes

Cynthia Mergen

Seven years ago, my Mama had a serious health event in December of 2016. During that time, I had just come back from a visit to my parents in Florida, where she had fallen seriously ill and needed hospitalization. Despite the initial grim outlook, she made a remarkable recovery during my stay and was transferred from the hospital to a rehabilitation center. Upon my return to Pennsylvania, I received a group text from my older brother advising all of us siblings to be available by phone. As the first to be called, a sense of fear enveloped me, anticipating tragic news.

"What is it?" was my response upon answering the phone. *"It's Dad. He's had a heart attack,"* he replied, sending a wave of pain through me. The fear of losing him loomed large, leading me into a whirlwind of thoughts and intercession.

After learning about Dad's condition, the rest of the conversation fades into a blur in my memory.

A few days later, I journeyed to Florida with one of my brothers, as Tom had prior commitments and would join us later. By this time, Papa was in an intensive care unit. Contrary to initial reports, he had not suffered a heart attack but a pulmonary embolism, requiring CPR to revive him. He was placed on life support due to his inability to breathe independently, and this marked the start of the most agonizing thirteen days of my life.

Each day, we were presented with contradictory medical updates. One group conveyed little optimism regarding brain activity, while another observed signs of activity in recent tests. With six siblings participating in the decision-making process, as difficult as it was, we decided to wait and see. Then our father's condition worsened, leading to the difficult choice to discontinue life support. Three agreed to proceed, while the remaining three preferred to wait, causing a split among us. Florida law stipulates that only 50% agreement is needed for such medical choices, leading the eldest three to grant permission for life support removal.

As the moment approached, the doctors offered us the choice to stay or bid farewell and depart. Each sibling took their turn to say goodbye, and when my turn came, I insisted, *"I will stay. I can't leave my father to pass alone."* I chose to remain by his side until his final breath. Moved by my decision, my eldest brother also chose to stay.

Every second leading up to our father's passing remains vivid in my memory. My brother, his wife, Tom, and I, accompanied by the hospital chaplain, watched as the medical team began the process of disconnecting life support. Overwhelmed, my sister-in-law left the room. The chaplain stood by my brother, offering comfort during this poignant moment.

Unexpectedly, the doctor surprised me by asking if I would like to sing to him. This was quite surprising since the doctor had never met me and had no prior knowledge that I was a singer. During my Papa's battle with cancer years ago, my siblings and I took turns going down to Florida to care for him and my mom for many weeks. When it was my turn to care for them, I sang worship songs and Nat King Cole tunes to him daily, both at home and in the hospital. These moments of intimacy shared with Papa hold a special place in my heart, as the palpable presence of love was all around us and felt within us.

> *...God is love, and whoever abides in love abides in God, and God abides in him.*
>
> 1 John 4:16, ESV

Later, I discovered he found solace and could sleep peacefully whenever I sang to him.

A nurse suggested I sing *Our Father* and offered to join me. There I stood before my Papa, eyes closed, pouring my heart into the song for both my Heavenly Father and my earthly father. As we sang together, our voices blended as one.

On December 20th, Papa passed away shortly after I sang to him with my hands over his heart. As I bid him farewell with a kiss, I whispered, *"I love you Papa, I'll love you forever!"* Tom stood nearby, silently comforting me with his touch. The chaplain embraced my eldest brother, offering words of encouragement. He expressed sensing a divine presence of God and a peace that defied understanding in the room. He shared that Papa had been the third "departure" of the day, and the presence of God was evident in a way he had not felt earlier in the day with other passings. These words brought me solace. We all felt the tangible presence of God as we witnessed the final moments of our father's life, as he transitioned into eternity. It was a blend of wonder and tragedy in one moment.

Something mystical occurred that night, and I was forever changed. At a later time, my brother shared how he sensed a profound connection between us as the only siblings present in the room. We experienced a bond words couldn't describe, drawing us closer as brother and sister.

On our way back to our Airbnb, we stopped at Publix to find something to eat. Though physically present, I was elsewhere in a spiritual realm. I observed my body moving and grabbing a food cart, with others noticing the same but remaining silent. Tom stayed by my side, guiding me through the store. Pushing a shopping cart at Publix after losing my father felt surreal. Without direction, I turned down an aisle.

I found myself in the snack aisle, with perfectly arranged shelves of various snacks and potato chips. It felt as though something guided me. As I pushed the cart, two large bags of potato chips suddenly fell in front of me, as if an invisible hand flicked them off the shelves causing them to land before me. At that moment, one of my elder brothers and his wife entered the aisle from the opposite end. She met us in the middle, and I spoke for the first time since leaving the hospital, asking, *"Did you see that?"* She confirmed, picked up one bag for herself, and placed the other in my cart. Potato chips were my father's favorite snack, and I truly believe it was a comforting sign from the Lord indicating Papa was in His presence. God's grace was truly remarkable that night, enveloping me with His divine presence. His kindness embraced me, guiding me through the days and weeks ahead.

Months prior, my father posed an unexpected question during a conversation. He asked, *"Daughter, if anything were to happen to me, what will become of Mom?"* Despite the emotional weight of his words, I reassured him, *"Don't worry, Papa, I will take care of Mama."* Content with my response, he replied, *"That's all I needed to hear, daughter,"* and swiftly shifted the conversation. It seemed as though he sensed his time on earth was drawing to a close.

As his passing approached, I grappled with the impending loss, never having witnessed someone's transition into eternity before. While our family had experienced loss previously, this was the first time I would witness it firsthand. Surrendering to the inevitable loss of my beloved Papa was a profound and heart-wrenching experience.

Following his passing, my husband Tom and I had to make a challenging journey by car of over 1200 miles back home to attend to our dogs, Zorro and Mickey, who were being cared for in a doggie hotel. Due to the holiday season, we needed to find temporary arrangements for them. Upon learning of my father's passing, the compassionate owner offered to take our dogs into her own home, allowing us to focus on arrangements for Papa's funeral and Mama's relocation to live with us.

Returning to Florida on Christmas Day, we discharged Mama from the hospital rehabilitation center, thus becoming her primary caregiver. Three days later, we held Papa's funeral, forever altering the essence of Christmas for us.

Nine months later, we experienced a similar ordeal when Mama joined Papa in glory. I sat by her side as she teetered between life and death. While Tom and my brother tended to tasks around the property, I remained by her side, silently praying and administering morphine to alleviate her pain.

As her breathing grew labored, I sought to comfort her, sensing her time was near. With a whisper, I reassured her, *"It's okay, Mama. Rest now. Go, be with Papa. I'll be fine."* Seconds later, she peacefully passed away, her final breath a poignant farewell.

The contrast in my reactions to Papa and Mama's passing was stark. While I remained composed at Papa's departure, Mama's passing evoked profound groans of grief and tears.

These experiences seemed insurmountable, shrouded in pain and sorrow. Yet, amidst the turmoil, I felt a peculiar sense of guidance, as if I were not entirely in control. Reflecting on those moments, I now recognize I was likely in a state of shock, unaware of the extent to which God was carrying me through it all. When Papa departed, it felt as though I had transcended my physical self, with an unseen force guiding me through each step. Being the only daughter and youngest among six siblings, I felt compelled to exude strength in their presence.

I knew God was with me as I purposed to lean on him heavily, yet I did not realize that I too needed to release the grief I had so carefully tucked away. Hence the release of the dam the moment Mama passed.

Not only was I focused on self-preservation, but I also felt the need to be a pillar of strength for my mother and extended family. After all, they were relying on me to take care of our mother.

Reflecting on the experience, I am grateful for the journey. It taught me how to navigate not only my own sorrow and feelings but also how to navigate through the diverse reactions to loss from each family member—a distinct challenge. Adversity can reveal our best and worst sides, and we must gracefully maneuver through it with as much wisdom, mercy, and grace as we can draw from our faith. This can only come from a place of intimacy. I understand firsthand how challenging it can be, particularly when you are experiencing such deep pain and sadness.

What does it mean to run to you, Father God? Can you help us let go of the fragments of our hearts we cling onto so tightly? The profound loss I experienced did not diminish His ability to fill those voids in my life.

I stopped seeking external solutions to fill a void I knew could never be satisfied by anyone else, though I craved a quick fix. Gradually, I began to trust and surrender to Jesus, understanding it was never intended for me or anyone to remain in a perpetual state of brokenness.

If I can't fully trust Him, how can I believe He genuinely brings healing and guides me toward complete wholeness? Letting go doesn't erase memories and love for those I've lost, but it does allow for healing from the sting of death and acceptance of a life filled with love, happiness, and restoration that comes from deepening my connection with him. This growth requires my roots to extend deeper.

Scripture tells us:

> Thus says the LORD, "Cursed is the man who trusts in and relies on mankind, making [weak, faulty human] flesh his strength, and whose mind and heart turn away from the LORD. "For he will be

> *like a shrub in the [parched] desert. And shall not see prosperity when it comes, But shall live in the rocky places of the wilderness, in an uninhabited salt land. "Blessed [with spiritual security] is the man who believes and trusts in and relies on the LORD and whose hope and confident expectation is the LORD. "For he will be [nourished] like a tree planted by the waters, That spreads out its roots by the river; and will not fear the heat when it comes; but its leaves will be green and moist. And it will not be anxious and concerned in a year of drought nor stop bearing fruit.*
>
> Jeremiah 17:5-8, AMP

I was beginning to understand now. This was the first inclination and beginning of what it must really mean to go deep. To surrender fully unto His leading. To trust, even when it felt I was too broken or grief-stricken, as if I'd lost my way. Only then could I fully realize the depth of who He is, on this side of glory.

I would be remiss if I didn't mention the series of losses we endured. Within a short span, we lost both my parents, followed closely by my husband Tom's father, just thirteen days after Mama passed. Tragically, four months prior to my Papa's passing, my eldest brother's son succumbed to cancer. This chain of events, involving four individuals in less than a year, was heartbreaking, and unfortunately, the sorrow didn't end there. Adding to our grief, our two beloved dogs, Mickey and Zorro, also passed away. Mickey passed a week after my mother, and Zorro, six months later. It felt like we were being hit repeatedly, and it was hard to see our way through.

Following my father's funeral, I moved my mother to Pennsylvania to live with us. As her health declined due to kidney failure and dementia, she required hospice care in my home. Focused on her needs and well-being, I set aside my own grief. Being her sole caregiver, I had to be strong for her—putting on a brave face to ease her suffering.

Reflecting on the past, I now realize the profound impact and divine setup of the circumstances by Abba. Despite our past differences, caring for my mother during her final nine months was the most humbling and profound chapter of my life. It was a period of reconciliation and healing, where we grew closer than ever before. Our relationship evolved, and she aptly remarked that our roles had reversed by saying, *"The daughter has become the mother, and the mother has become the daughter."* I discovered a newfound love for her as I learned about her past, despite the dementia, and gained a newfound understanding of who she really is. I speak in the present tense because, to me, they remain alive in spirit. Those who have passed are living on in glory, and I know one day we will be together again.

After some time had passed, Tom and I tried to get some semblance of hope for our life and future, and we began to see the clouds dissipate and some light before us. During this time, our niece Stefanee came from the West to live with us for a season as she pursued a career on the East Coast. She is a wonderfully vibrant young woman, and we were blessed to have her with us.

Who could have ever imagined during this glimpse of hope and semblance of normality, tragedy would strike again?

When April 1, 2019 came, it ushered in the loss of my husband Tom's elder sister Cheryl, who passed away after a difficult battle with lung cancer. Just seven days later, my brother Steven was tragically taken from us in a motor vehicle accident. He was also Stefanee's father. There simply are no words to describe the shock and dismay we all felt on that dreadful day. In a time span of 3 years, my family lost 6 people and 2 beloved dogs.

I literally thought, "What was God thinking?!" as so many others did when they expressed shock and dismay over this senseless tragedy. I had reached my breaking point. It was incomprehensible, and I felt completely and utterly alone.

Grief is indescribable, and it's different for each one of us. Its effects carry a weight piercing the heart with no mercy.

For me, it became all too real when I realized this path had only room for one set of footprints, and while it feels like you don't know how to recover, somehow, you lean into Abba, start to let go, and begin to learn how to breathe again. Then, little by little, you trust God to carry you until you can walk again.

Once again, autopilot in the form of Holy Spirit took over. I may not have known then during it all, but I realize it now.

Thankfully, God's ways are higher than our ways as He saw to it that I would be tethered to Him. The Comforter had brought heaven to earth in such a way to help and guide me to a deeper level of comprehension. As I stepped into it, an inner strength began to rise, releasing a healing I previously had no grid for. His grace and mercy were evident in a way I cannot describe but to say it is never-ending, always renewing, always patient and kind, despite my ability or inability to contain it. Abba changed that in me. This brings clarity to the scriptures in Luke, which says:

> *"And no one puts new wine into old wineskins; otherwise, the new (fermenting) wine will (expand and) burst the skins and it will be spilled out, and the skins will be ruined. But new wine must be put into fresh wineskins."*
>
> Luke 5:37-38, AMP

A joy unimaginable became evident. It broke over us, in such a way it changed the atmosphere around us as it began to spill over into our home. While it may not have happened overnight, it ushered in a peace I have yet to find words for along with comfort knowing I will not only see those we've lost again, but I will walk knowing that we are His, and our life here on earth has a distinct and divine purpose.

THE REFINING FIRE

Our journey began to lead Tom and me down a path that caused a movement of things Abba wanted to work out in us. I was being led to a desolate place where he began to slough off the things he no longer wanted me to carry. All the things I had set my gaze upon thinking they were of Him, yet they were not.

This quickly transitioned into a place where everything past, present, and future was on the chopping block via refining fire, which meant anyone or anything not meant to go with me, or would hinder the transition of being refined by fire, had to be dealt with and removed.

It began with those things I placed value on and the relationships that had waned through the testing of time. These were the ones where the common bond was born from a wound and a binding together out of a place of need rather than a place of assignment or calling. If these relationships were indeed appointed by God, the trying times we would face would only strengthen the bonds among the Ekklesia as we rise and align as one body.

Sometimes there are those along the course of life we simply attach ourselves to. Some relationships are God-appointed, while others can result from a season of woundedness and like-mindedness. If we are not careful, we can form bonds with others from a place of need and dependence, rather than a divine purpose. Such relationships can lead us down a path away from what God intended. They can distract and lead you away from the perfect course God has for us as the open wounds of an orphan spirit begin to bleed you dry of your divine destiny. Ultimately, we must die to self, and seek the higher purpose. It's important for me to place a disclaimer here as I am not targeting any one person—just merely extrapolating from my experience through life. We must use wisdom, while walking in love, always being obedient to God's leading and direction first and discern how to navigate relationships through God's lenses and not our own. As we grow and go low in Jesus, He will make clear those we are appointed to run with.

> *"It takes a grinding wheel to sharpen a blade, and so one person sharpens the character of another."*
>
> Proverbs 27:17, TPT

A New Order of Things

One year after our sibling's passing, COVID-19 hit the world, and fear gripped our nation as we all went on lockdown. Tom and I live in the country and are used to small-town living. We had literally just come through three years of hell and grief on Earth, so for us, this seemed like a cakewalk.

I found a community of believers online and on social media that helped sustain me for a time. We began to have Zoom calls and meetings, and God was moving greatly. I began to feel a newness of life and purpose again and found joy in the fact God was not only moving, but He was also moving through and in me. God had ushered in the release of a new realm of His presence and joy literally swept the nation.

Looking back, I realize through all our suffering, the most crucial thing Tom and I were determined to do was run to Him. We'd lived through what seemed a lifetime of loss and tragedy, yet by God's providence, his enduring love swept in and covered us with an indescribable amount of grace. A grace I never really understood until I was crushed like grapes, bringing me to the end of myself. It didn't happen overnight. No matter how difficult the journey, He somehow lifts you up and over. The apostle Paul writes it so eloquently:

> *"...because I know that the lavish supply of the Spirit of Jesus, the Anointed One, and your intercession for me will bring about my deliverance. No matter what, I will continue to hope and passionately cling to Christ, so that he will be openly revealed through me before everyone's eyes. So, I will not be ashamed! In my life or in my death, Christ will be magnified in me. My true life is the Anointed One, and dying means gaining more of him."*
>
> Philippians 1:19-21, TPT

There is no timeline for this. It depends on two things—God's providence, and one's ability and willingness to go deeper than our human understanding and emotions may allow. We must fully trust and completely surrender the deepest parts of our very being.

Bill Johnson once said these very words while preaching three days after his wife's passing:

"You see, you've got a mourning that leads you to Him and a mourning that leads us to a resistance to the God who is actually speaking and reaching out to us, bringing us the gift of life and encouragement, and strength in this journey that I'm in right now."

Those words pierced my heart in a powerful way because I understood the true meaning of his message.

This point in my story would seem like a perfect time to say how we've crossed a bridge and come out of the other side unscathed, but that was not our reality.

THE DESOLATE PLACE

Just as the dust had settled, and there was a glimpse of some normality, I was actively serving in a women's group throughout the duration of lockdown and COVID-19, when things began to shift again. I began to feel exhausted supernaturally and physically when I suddenly felt my assignment was being shaken. As things began to shift, I was struggling with what I was sensing in my spirit. I began to clearly hear these words, *"I am leading you into a place of rest."*

At the time, I felt Holy Spirit was leading me to resign but felt conflicted as I had worked so hard as a volunteer for this organization for approximately two years. I had a genuine love for its vision and the friendships that were forged. I struggled to cope with the notion that God wanted access to all I held dear, just like Abraham's testing with Isaac. Little did I know as I held on to hope for a bright and prosperous future, near tragedy had unbelievably struck again.

On Christmas Eve of 2021, I fell seriously ill and had to be rushed to the hospital. After nearly two years of evading it, COVID-19 had finally caught up with us.

It began with Tom testing positive, followed by me several days later. While Tom quickly recovered, my condition worsened.

An ambulance transported me to the ER, but with the hospital at full capacity, the EMTs anticipated redirecting us to a facility about 50 minutes away. In silent prayer to Jesus for intervention, a nurse suddenly directed the EMTs to follow her. Passing by numerous patients in medical distress, I was led to a room for immediate care in a newly opened hospital. Following tests and multiple IVs, I was diagnosed with COVID pneumonia as my organs, in addition to my lungs, were under attack.

Around the fifth day, the doctor showed me a CT scan revealing one lung completely affected and the other 70% compromised. Due to the treatment's ineffectiveness, the doctor suggested moving me to the ICU for intubation, even presenting a DNR form he wanted me to sign. Determined not to give up, I called my husband who had already been informed. With renewed faith, I refused to sign my own death warrant, believing survival was within reach. I spoke up as best I could through the high-flow oxygen cannula and said the following words:

"You are not moving me to ICU, and you will not intubate me, and no, I will not sign a DNR! Outside of these stipulations, do your part, and I'll trust Jesus for the rest. I choose life, and my God will heal me!"

With that, they left the room.

The following day, my dedicated nurse arrived with treatments and a comforting cup of tea. She took great care of me, undoubtedly a blessing. At one point, a close friend from Texas called and prophesied that an angel in the form of a nurse would be sent to watch over and care for me. It became clear to me she was indeed that person. Besides managing all the IV treatments and medications, she applied medical cream to ease the intense pain I was experiencing. Additionally, she massaged essential oils from my head down the center of my spine every morning and night, as per my instructions. One evening, she confided in me about the doctor who had spoken to me the night before, revealing he was the top internal medicine specialist in our region despite his lacking bedside manner.

Her words reassured me, and she emphasized the severity of my condition by mentioning another patient with the same COVID pneumonia a few doors down who had been hospitalized for 7 weeks. She went on to say my lungs looked worse than his. I confidently responded, *"That's okay, God will heal me anyway!"* miraculously my faith was high, despite the medical staff persistently presenting me with Do Not Resuscitate (DNR) papers for three consecutive days until I firmly asked them to stop.

Somewhere in the middle of my stay, I had an encounter with God. Whether I dreamed it, had a visitation, or was taken up, I cannot say. All I know is I found myself out of my body, and in a very dark place. I went down low and reached a place that appeared to be a dark alley. I fearfully knew it to be a place of death. It was grayish dark all around me, as if everything was in black and white. A series of events transpired as I was then caught up in a heavenly place which I am not at liberty to reveal here.

I found myself within the embrace of the Almighty and was brought close. I heard these words in my ear, *"Drop your sword for the battle is not yours, it is mine. Trust me and lean into me, and I will heal you!"* A tremendous peace came upon me, and I knew I had just received a divine touch and instruction from the Lord. Now, stick with me for a moment. I know what scripture says about the sword of the spirit, yet this is what I heard and did not question it. Later, I began to see I was not wielding correctly what I thought to be my sword. I was fighting in my own strength a battle only God could win, while believing I was standing on biblical principle.

> *"...Not by might, nor by power, but by my Spirit, says the Lord of hosts."*
>
> Zechariah 4:6, ESV

The next thing I recall is waking up back in my hospital bed with a nurse urgently calling my name. She apologized for the delay in responding to the alarms in my room. It turned out my high-flow oxygen cannula had slipped off, causing my oxygen saturation levels to dangerously decrease. As she reconnected me to the oxygen supply, I gazed at her in silence and drifted off to sleep.

In the days that followed, my room became a place of continuous worship. I started and ended my day with worship and eagerly awaited the nighttime hours when I would be caught up whilst asleep into the heavenly places.

Friends and family from across the country joined me via Zoom one night. Each one took their turn praying for me and any staff who entered the room. I was surrounded by love, praise, and worship around the clock, even though visitors were not permitted. I was certain God would not abandon me and remained steadfast in my faith, refusing to accept any negative reports. Every night, I felt His presence lifting me to heavenly realms, revealing secrets I could not articulate.

I chose to embrace life, and my faith was rewarded as I placed my trust in God.

Another cherished memory was when I saw my husband's smile through the window, despite visitor restrictions. He defied the rules to visit me on the second floor, bringing tears to my eyes with his loving words about how beautiful I looked even though I had been at death's door.

Later, the doctor who delivered the grim news to me came back with a heartfelt apology. He admitted I was the worst case, but miraculously, it turned out to be the best outcome. With tears rolling down, I prayed for him, speaking words of life and forgiveness that deeply touched him. He was overcome by the power of Holy Spirit spouting, *"Such powerful words I have never heard. You have no idea how much this means to me!"* I was discharged on a snowy January day, weak and almost voiceless from illness.

Over the following months, I needed intensive therapy and care at home due to Long Covid Syndrome. As I gradually regained strength, I faced challenges like losing my hair and needing oxygen equipment round the clock, symbolizing a new chapter in my journey. Despite the hardships, I held onto faith, trusting God's plan and His guidance through the refining process toward holiness. The battle, both physical and spiritual, was intense, pushing me to my limits and stripping away what I once knew. This struggle became a transformative journey, leading me to a place of deeper faith and resilience.

This was the fight for my life. The fight that would get me to the highest place by going even lower than I had the capacity for. But God. The physical battle to wholeness was great, but the spiritual battle to holiness was far greater.

Bringing Beauty out of Ashes

Through multiple tragedies, the loss of loved ones, and rehabilitating throughout 2022 and 2023 from C19 Pneumonia while facing subsequent health issues have taught me the essence of what it is to fully rest, refresh, and restore. Guided by Holy Spirit's refining fire towards holiness, I've embraced a lifestyle centered on Him via rest, and altering my perception of God and His plans for me.

I would like to end by leaving you with these final thoughts:

- By allowing room for personal and spiritual growth, we will find ourselves shedding old wineskins and entering a transformative rejuvenation of the new wineskin.

- When we earnestly pray to become more like Him, we will most certainly be taken through a refining fire process.

- Sharing my experience of loss and near-death encounters aims to offer hope and direction to those struggling with loss and grief.

- For those grappling with long-standing emotional wounds, may you find solace in God's healing love.

- Take heart. "...*Weeping may last through the night, but joy comes with the morning.*" (Psalm 30:5, NLT)

- Surrendering to His grace appoints holy relationships for the journey, fostering trust and companionship.

- Finding comfort in mourning involves surrender, consolation,

BREAKING INTO BROKENNESS-BRINGING BEAUTY OUT OF...

encouragement, and earnest guidance even when we don't understand it.

- God transforms beauty from the ashes, embodying the role of Jehovah Rophe—The Lord My Healer.

> *"When they are sick, lying upon their bed of suffering, God will restore them. He will raise them up again and restore them back to health. So in my sickness I say to you, "Lord, be my kind healer. Heal my body and soul; heal me, God! For I have confessed my sins to you."*
> Psalm 41:3-4, TPT

In the midst of profound breakthroughs catalyzed by God's enduring love, I embarked on a journey of profound inner healing that transcended natural means.

- It commences with surrender and unfolds with divine appointments for support along the way.

- *"Blessed are those who mourn, for they shall be comforted."* (Matthew 5:4, NKJV)

- In the depths of despair, we often encounter aspects of God's presence that illuminate His kindness and miraculous interventions.

- Through the transformative journey, God restores what is broken and brings *forth beauty from ashes*.

> *"...he will give a crown of beauty for ashes, a joyous blessing instead of mourning, festive praise instead of despair. In their righteousness, they will be like great oaks that the LORD has planted for his own glory."*
> Isaiah 61:3 NLT

- Freely receive God's role as the Father of compassion and the source of eternal comfort.

"All praises belong to the God and Father of our Lord Jesus Christ. For he is the Father of tender mercy and the God of endless comfort. He always comes alongside us to comfort us in every suffering so that we can come alongside those who are in any painful trial. We can bring them this same comfort that God has poured out upon us."

2 Corinthians 1:3-4, TPT

- James 1 reminds us to find joy in trials, as they refine our faith and lead to spiritual maturity.

"Dear brothers and sisters, when troubles of any kind come your way, consider it an opportunity for great joy. For you know that when your faith is tested, your endurance has a chance to grow. So let it grow, for when your endurance is fully developed, you will be perfect and complete, needing nothing."

James 1:2-4, NLT

May the same grace and presence that sustained me over the past seven years envelop you, bringing healing and comfort to your every wound and sorrow.

Remember, when challenges arise, God will provide a way through and stand with you against adversity.

Let the floodgates of heaven open, for His presence will be with you always.

About the Author

Cynthia Mergen has a compelling testimony of healing breakthroughs and deliverance after enduring multiple family tragedies and a challenging illness. She is an experienced prophetic intercessor, speaker, writer, gifted psalmist, teacher, and kingdom leader. As the co-founder of Heaven to Earth Life, she is called to nations to bring transformative healing to the Body of Christ.

With dedication, Cynthia has held leadership positions in churches, ministries, and various non-profit organizations emphasizing breakthroughs, love, and the healing power of Jesus Christ.

Cynthia also serves as an inner healing breakthrough facilitator and team member at Sent Ones Ministries under the remarkable leadership of its founders, Josh and Maria Adkins.

She resides in Pennsylvania with her husband Tom, niece Stefanee, and their fun-loving dogs, Penny and Jackson.